Small Is
Bountiful

Small Is
Bountiful

Getting More Crops from Your Pots

Liz Dobbs with **Anne Halpin**

Reader's
Digest

The Reader's Digest Association, Inc.
New York, NY/Montreal

A READER'S DIGEST BOOK

The edition published by The Reader's Digest Association, Inc.
by arrangement with Toucan Books Ltd.

FOR TOUCAN BOOKS
Project Designer Mark Scribbins
Project Editor Theresa Bebbington
Managing Editor Ellen Dupont
Proofreader Marion Dent
Indexer Marie Lorimer
Photo Researcher Sharon Southren

FOR READER'S DIGEST
U.S. Project Editor Kim Casey
Canadian Project Editor Robert Ronald
Manager, English Book Editorial Reader's Digest Canada Pamela Johnson
Project Designer Jennifer Tokarski
Senior Art Director George McKeon
Editor-in-Chief, Books & Home Entertainment Neil Wertheimer
Associate Publisher Rosanne McManus
President and Publisher, Trade Publishing Harold Clarke

Library of Congress Cataloging-in-Publication Data
Dobbs, Liz, 1958-
  Small is bountiful : getting more crops from your pots / Liz Dobbs with Anne Halpin. -- 1st ed.
       p. cm.
  Includes index.
  ISBN 978-1-60652-420-6
  1. Patio gardening. 2. Container gardening. 3. Small gardens. I. Halpin, Anne Moyer. II. Title. III. Title: Getting more crops from your pots.
  SB473.2.D63 2012
  635--dc23
                        2011027814

For more Reader's Digest products and information, visit our website:
    www.rd.com (in the United States)
    www.readersdigest.ca (in Canada)

Printed in China

1 3 5 7 9 10 8 6 4 2

Contents

Introduction

No garden? No problem! All you need are a few suitable containers and the right plants. You can grow some of your own food, even if you only have a small outdoor space without any garden soil.

Planting some attractive vegetable plants close to your home and growing them with ornamental flowers can be both practical and beautiful. You'll love picking fresh herbs every day from just outside the kitchen door—they will be so easy to reach when cooking. You can move the containers around, showing them off at their prime and moving them to a less conspicuous spot when they are at their least attractive. It will also be easier to move them away from nibbling critters or to bring them inside if it gets too cold outside.

Even if you have a large yard, you may still want to grow vegetables in containers if most of your yard is too shady. On the other hand, if your outdoor space is limited to just a balcony, front porch, or even a roof garden, growing vegetables in containers is often the only option available. However, there are more choices than you might have considered, such as using vertical spaces for pouches of fresh herbs.

This book aims to offer both inspiration and practical advice, showcasing the best plants to grow in a wide range of containers, from hanging baskets to large planters. There are 34 projects that look as good as they taste and detailed growing advice for more than 40 different vegetables, herbs, and edible flowers. Even if you have never grown anything before, planting a few herbs or salad

A flowerpot with rosemary and orange marigolds is an attractive planting suitable for a patio setting with other plants or on its own, perhaps near a kitchen door.

A mixed planting includes French tarragon and red begonias, with frilly-leaved red lettuce making charming edging plants.

into three groups. Small Bites covers the fast crops, such as leafy greens and herbs. These will grow in smaller pots or in planting arrangements that look pretty enough to sit on the deck, yet still yield plenty of edibles. Next Bigger Servings looks at increasing the harvest by growing plants in larger planters. Last but not least, the focus on Going UP! is to make the most of vertical space to grow crops, whether it be window boxes of chilies, walls of flowering green beans, or hanging baskets full of tomatoes.

Why not try some bowls of Speedy Stir-Fry on a patio table, a planter of strawberries on a wall ledge, or a planter of potatoes. The recipes will provide plenty of inspiration—no matter the size of your space. All the details are there for you to re-create the plantings with confidence or use them to inspire your own ideas. Some plants, such as herbs, tomatoes, and zucchini, are so prolific that you will probably have more than you can eat. To help you use your bounty, there are recipes with the relevant plantings.

Violas add a cheerful splash in a sea of green lettuce. However, there's another reason to grow these annuals— the petals are also edible.

greens in containers is a great place to start, and you will be able to enjoy and eat the results within one season. Even gardeners who are familiar with combining flowers and foliage in containers for ornamental displays will find some fresh ideas for being creative with edible plants.

The plantings

The projects have been developed around "recipes," where we've put together plantings based on how you would use the harvest in the kitchen, whether it is a Taste of Italy, which provides tomato with basil to make bruschetta, or to have a mixture of mint available to pick. These planting recipes have been divided

Big Ideas for Small Spaces

One of the challenges of growing in a small space is to get as much as possible from it. When you plant a container with edible plants, also consider how to add something extra. Could you, for example, add some annual flowers or herbs for color and also to attract beneficial insects? Or could you squeeze in another quick-growing plant, such as lettuce or spinach, before or after the main plantings? Here's a selection of our favorite ideas for getting the most out of small spaces, grouped by container size and location.

11

Small Bites

If you already plant a few flowerpots each spring with annuals to add summer color to an outdoor space, all you need to do is adapt them. However, even if you don't have flowerpots, you can soon be planting your own fresh edibles.

The flowerpots and planters normally used for annuals are also suitable for producing a selection of tasty edibles. For example, in smaller containers under 16 inches (40 cm) in diameter, you can grow several baskets full of tomatoes or chilies. At the least, you can have a daily supply of salad greens, handfuls of fresh herbs, stir-fry greens, and edible flowers for garnishes and herbal teas.

Apart from buying edible plants alongside your ornamentals, you won't need to invest in much more. The essentials are potting mix, slug control, and watering equipment—which is just the same as for flowers. You will also need to purchase a balanced all-purpose fertilizer and a tomato fertilizer to increase your harvest.

Plant selection

For the biggest yield, grow vegetables in their own containers so there is less competition from other plants. However, choose plants that are ornamental, such as Swiss chard, chilies, or mixed lettuce. Alternatively, place ornamentals in other flowerpots alongside your vegetables. For example, use three glazed terra-cotta pots, each slightly smaller than the other. Plant a vegetable crop, such as beans, in the largest one, a salad green or herb in the middle one, and an ornamental in the smallest one; then arrange them to make an attractive display. Be sure the larger plant is north of the smaller ones so it doesn't cast a shadow on them. If you have little space, you can grow vegetables and ornamentals together in one container, but you will have to compromise on your plant selection. Mixed herbs and edible flowers in the same container will work well because you will be picking smaller quantities.

Some modern varieties of vegetables, salad greens, and herbs are a better choice for container growing because they are more compact or colorful, or they mature faster, than older types. Tomato plants, for example, were originally straggling vines, but there are now varieties available in a wide range of habits, or shapes, from cascades for hanging baskets to squat bushes. Even a single chili plant sitting on your table could give you more than

Colorful Swiss chard (above) makes an attractive display. Try planting them in a mixture of different containers and grouping them together.

A single planting of chilies (right) can supply enough peppers for the whole family—and also creates a festive focal point.

enough peppers and there are few prettier plants. Basil is an herb that has a lot of breeding work, and there are now selections in a range of leaf sizes and colors—not to mention some attractive flowering ones. Quick-maturing vegetable varieties from loose-leaf lettuce to Asian greens to the humble radish mean that you can be serving fresh food from seeds within five weeks—even small spaces can be productive.

A room outdoors

If you have a sitting or entertaining area outside, chances are it is in a warm, sheltered spot near the house or at least within easy access. Most edibles will crop much better in a sunny, sheltered

A mixture of leaf shapes and textures adds interest to this grouping of vegetables and herbs, which includes Swiss chard, sage, and basil, along with flowering nasturtiums.

position than in a dark corner or in a cold, windy place. For the best results, it makes sense to place containers on the patio or deck. As an added bonus, you will find it easier to remember to provide them with the daily attention they need and to notice when they are ready for picking.

Off the ground

Outdoor features, from tabletops to benches, are suitable positions for small containers, which will keep them away from slugs and snails. Sow shallow bowls with mixed lettuce or Asian greens, and they will crop in about five weeks. Several herbs, such as prostrate rosemary, variegated sage, and thyme, also do well in shallow bowls. Sit them on a matching drip tray to keep the tabletop clean, but don't let their roots sit in water. Benches are useful places for hardening off young plants early in the season, because you can drape a floating row cover over them. Low, wide walls are handy for potatoes growing in bags, carrots in flowerpots, or windowbox planters filled with salad greens, herbs, and bush tomatoes. The top of storage units— for example, for bicycles or firewood—are ideal for planters of mixed herbs.

Beds and borders

Most beds and borders have space either at the front or gaps between plants, usually at the start of the season or toward

Arrange a grouping of containers with a selection of herbs, such as thyme, basil, and chives, along with different types of lettuce.

the end, when plants have been cut back. Beds mulched with gravel can be a handy temporary home for pots of hardy herbs in late spring to early summer. In early fall, once the front plants have been cut back, a row of flowerpots with chilies, parsley, or thyme, for example, will add color. An obelisk with pole beans and nasturtiums weaving through it adds both color and crops. Where the soil is bare, you can put down a paving slab to support the container. Remember to water and feed the plants, and protect them from slugs and snails.

Back doors and hidden corners

You can use locations that are not normally on display—for example, outside the kitchen door, passageways, or under a tree—for growing food, but you should be realistic. Although a collection of herb plants outside the kitchen door might be handy for picking, if it is a cold, damp, and shady spot, the plants will not thrive. In a shaded area, try some woodland herbs in flowerpots, such as mint or parsley, leafy salad greens, or even a container of potatoes. At least growing vegetables and herbs in small containers means you can move them into a sunny space every now and then.

When choosing "found" planters, make sure their size is suitable for the plants, such as this deep bread box for short carrot varieties.

 Grow for it!

Ornamentals for a color boost

- These flowers need sun but can cope with a dryish potting mix: marguerite daisy, gazania, geranium, petunia, and zinnia.
- Flowers that tolerate partial shade and moist potting mix include alyssum, begonia, lobelia, impatiens, small fuchsias, and French marigold.
- Two attractive foliage fillers are coleus and heuchera. Also look for variegated versions of culinary herbs and geranium to provide extra color.

Out the front

If your front yard gets more sun than the backyard, why not use that space? You might want privacy, but your tomatoes will not mind passersby. Because you will be going in and out of the front door each day, you will be prompted to care for the plants. If you have a front porch or veranda, it could also provide enough extra shelter to make a difference in giving the plants an early start. Look for containers and plants that complement your building's style. They don't necessarily have to be bold—understated containers and plantings of herbs, vegetables, and annuals may be more suitable to your surroundings and tastes than bright, colorful ones.

Bigger Servings

An increase in container size will considerably broaden your growing horizons, letting you grow a complete complement of vegetables and herbs with enough to preserve and store.

Increasing the size of a container to a minimum of 18 inches (45 cm) in diameter will provide enough space for growing more than one type of edible plant. A larger container will also hold more volume, so you can grow root crops, such as potatoes, carrots, and beets, to a more mature size for storage. Vines and climbers, from zucchini and cucumbers to tomatoes to pole beans, will be more manageable when it comes to watering and support, and often even only a couple of these plants will be enough to supply a family all summer. Although you can grow leafy salad greens and herbs in smaller flowerpots, they are much more productive in larger containers; in fact, you can be self-sufficient in salad greens and have enough herbs to harvest and preserve for a winter supply.

Because there is a larger volume to surface area ratio, the potting mix will be less susceptible to the extremes of waterlogging, then drying out, and there is less risk of the roots getting too hot in summer. There will also be less day-to-day care when growing vegetables in larger containers.

Productive or pretty?

Before acquiring the materials you will need and setting up the plantings, first plan ahead. Is your priority to get a large harvest of potatoes or tomatoes? In that case, these container plantings will not be as attractive as a mixture of edible flowers or herbs, although a cook will be able to do more with a planter or two of potatoes or tomatoes than flowers. You can fit potato plants in woven, sturdy plastic bags or planters among more ornamental containers. A good tip is to grow them in black containers at the back because they will be less noticeable than white or bright, colorful ones. Or you can move containers to a less prominent position; this is handy with larger tomato plants that start to look scraggly just when they have the most tomatoes on them.

Square-shaped containers provide more room for mixed plantings (left), such as these herbs. This attractive planter draws the eyes away from the plain pots used behind it for the taller vegetables.

Plain, deep pots and bags have been hidden by placing them inside more attractive, square wicker covers (right).

Round flowerpots and recycled materials

Large, conventional clay flowerpots can be expensive, so be prepared to think laterally. For example, plastic planters or recycled containers, such as wooden apple crates, metal olive oil cans, or old preserving pans, can be suitable. If using wooden crates, first line them with plastic (make slits for drainage holes). Or use them to hold a group of pots of vegetables or herbs. Plastic buckets and laundry baskets are inexpensive, light, and easy to move around. Laundry baskets, lined with plastic, if necessary, will hold a few zucchini plants, but add some nasturtiums or marigolds for color. Don't take chances with your health by growing your edibles in recycled containers that once held chemicals—use only containers previously used for food or safe domestic situations.

Always position large pots and containers in their final location before filling them with potting mix. For potato or strawberry planters, ones with handles are useful if you need to move them to protect from frost or birds. A plant trolley, wheelbarrow, or even a skateboard will help move heavy containers or consider attaching casters to wooden or plastic containers.

A metal planter with a mixed planting of both red and green bok choy, climbing beans, and a feathery bronze fennel makes an attractive feature, replacing a bed in a very small yard.

Manger-style planters make good use of space in a small yard. Put plants that need greater root depth in the center.

Linear planters

Large, square or rectangular planters make better use of space near buildings or features defined by straight lines and corners than round flowerpots. They suit a courtyard, patio, deck, porch, veranda, balcony, or roof garden. A pair of square planters, one on each side of an entrance or at the top of steps, for example, could be formal with a standard bay tree clipped into shape and underplanted with neat thyme. Planters are useful for growing a short row of crops, and a line of planters alongside a sunny garage wall with trellis supports can supply you with a crop of pole beans, with lettuce or spinach tucked in between. They are also useful for strawberries, because you can get more plants in them than in pots and baskets, and they are easier to cover with netting to protect them from birds. On a balcony or roof garden, plastic and fiberglass planters come into their own, often doubling up as screens to provide privacy.

Special planters are available for growing a large quantity of tomatoes, sweet peppers, or cucumbers in a small space with the minimum of mess. These self-contained systems have a built-in water reservoir—so there is no leaking onto a deck, for example—and there are attached supports for the plants. The container has wheels so the whole thing can be moved out of the way.

Containers with wheels, such as this Earthbox, are useful for moving large containers safely around your outdoor space.

Size with style

In a small yard where the containers are always visible, you can invest in one or two large elegant ones and fill them with a mixture of vegetables or herbs to make a feature of them. They are almost a substitute for a border or bed, and you can make them more so by planting some herbs at the bottom corners to anchor in the planting. For a mixture of vegetables and herbs, start with a tall or architectural subject—such as corn or a sweet pepper—then plant some smaller subjects, such as lettuce or parsley. Finally, add a bit of color or a trailing plant, like a flowering herb, such as chives or basil, or a colorful annual. Make sure you have a few extra plants waiting in the wings to fill the space after harvesting the main crop.

Raised beds

After a certain point, a particularly large planter might as well be a raised bed. There is no precise measurement that can signal when to switch from containers to a raised bed, but consider a raised bed when it gets too expensive to buy enough containers, or when they are too heavy or cumbersome to move. A raised bed is usually, but not always, in contact with the ground beneath, forming four sides for holding topsoil and well-rotted organic compost. Raised bed kits are available in plastic, metal, or wood. Most are modular and come with accessories, such as hoops, for supporting floating row covers. You can also make your own from sawn wood.

Potato plants provide plenty of green foliage but few flowers, so place them where they won't need to be the center of attention.

 Grow for it!

Flowers for after the harvest

- After potatoes have been harvested, the leftover potting mix can be reused; for example, it is perfect for planting tulip bulbs in fall. When spring arrives, add lettuce and a tarragon; then remove the tulips after flowering and replace with bedding plants around the lettuce and tarragon.
- Ornamental perennials, such as agapanthus, day lilies, fuchsia, showy sedum, or dwarf rudbeckia, can replace crops harvested early to midsummer. Plant the perennials in the center and plant low-growing herbs around the edge for a display into fall.

Going UP!

By simply adding a basket of tomato plants hanging from your porch, you are practicing "vertical" gardening. Look up and around to see what other growing spaces you have—perhaps a sunny wall or fence—then select containers for planting.

Traditional planters, such as hanging baskets, wall planters, and window boxes, are ideal for tomatoes, chilies, bush beans, and lettuce as well as herbs and edible flowers. Some planters have extra features to make vertical gardening easier, such as containers shaped to fit over the tops of railings, baskets with built-in water reservoirs, and window boxes that come with inner liners so you can easily swap a tired harvested planting for fresh new plants. If you position planters above head height, you will need to be sure they are well secured with brackets of the appropriate size and strength.

Climbing success

Attractive and bountiful pole bean plants make excellent use of vertical space. The plants can grow in the

Grow pole beans up a pergola (left) for a summer screen, colorful flowers, and supply of beans.

These rustic-looking window boxes (opposite) have liners inside them, so the display can be changed during the season.

ground or in a large flowerpot or planter. For support, use either a temporary tepee of stakes or grow the plants against a permanent structure, such as a trellis, fence, or pergola, mixing them in with ornamental annual climbers, such as morning glories.

Wall space

You can attach new innovations, such as flexible planting pouches or pockets, to walls to "green" them. The most advanced ones are modular systems with a built-in automatic irrigation system that can be assembled to create something to fit within your space. These planters take up little room and create exciting opportunities for growing food in a courtyard or a balcony. An expanse of plants

---

 Grow for it!

Plants for high places

- For sunny surfaces where watering can be difficult, choose plants that can tolerate dry conditions; these include some herbs, such as thyme, sage, dwarf lavender, oregano, and a small rosemary.

- Sun with a moist medium provides the ideal site for strawberries, bush or tumbling tomatoes, or a crop of bush beans or bush peas.

- For partial shade with a moist medium, choose parsley, chives, loose-leaf lettuce varieties, and arugula. To make a really pretty display, you can add violas.

on vertical surfaces, particularly in urban areas, cools the interior and surroundings in summer.

On a practical note, hanging baskets work well where ground space is limited. However, you also need to be sure their containers do not protrude along walkways. Wind is a challenge for the plants, and you will see them wilt if the roots cannot supply the leaves with enough water to replace the amount lost by wind. Make sure the plants have grown enough so their roots are holding the potting mix together before arranging them, and harden off plants well (see page 107) before putting them into their final positions. Finally, make sure the plants will have a sufficient water supply.

Hanging baskets and wall planters

For your first baskets, or if you have little time, try the more modern designs of wicker or coir lined with plastic; you just need to position the plants at the top, unlike other types in which they are inserted in the sides. Include one or two trailing plants, even if these are not edible, to soften the display. There are now hybrid containers that are a cross between a basket and a plant pouch. They can be awkward to plant, but they look attractive once the plants have covered the container, and they usually have a water reservoir. Wall planters are more ornamental than productive, but a group of three glazed pots arranged on a wall can supply some fresh herbs. Use small drought-tolerant herbs, such as thyme, dwarf lavender, and chives, plus a garlic or even a dwarf chili.

Not much will grow under a mature shady tree, but it does provide an opportunity to hang a basket of loose-leaf lettuce, which prefers protection from the sun during a hot summer.

 Grow for it!

Trailing flowers

- Edible plants that trail include tumbler-type tomatoes, trailing nasturtiums, and trailing violas.
- There is a wider range of nonedible annuals with flowers that last all summer; choose from *Bacopa cordata*, *Sanvitalia procumbens*, and trailing varieties of begonia, bidens, calibrachoa, fuchsia, petunia, and verbena.
- Foliage trailing plants add color, too; for example, *Dichondra* 'Silver Falls' and a silver-leaved helichrysum both provide silver foliage. A sweet potato vine offers ornamental foliage in 'Sweetheart Purple'.

Balconies and boundaries

Despite their name, window boxes can also be fitted to the sides of balconies. The ideal place is in a sunny spot that you can reach safely and near a water supply. Also remember the importance of secure fittings. Some containers are designed to straddle balconies, with the potting mix weighing them down in place. Drainage holes are vital, but after watering, the potting mix can be washed through and leave a mess. Line the container with newspaper; it will slowly disintegrate, but by then the potting mix will be held in place by the roots. Or use plastic containers with built-in reservoirs. Fencing or trellis screens can become productive by using plant pouches or hook-on wooden shelves. Or attach brackets for hanging baskets to fence posts.

Wide steps provide an opportunity for growing cucumbers with attractive yellow flowers. This variety forms round cucumbers.

Stages and steps

Display shelves with tiers can hold a number of small flowerpots, offering a taste of herbs and salad greens, as well as color from chilies and tiny tomatoes. The simplest are wooden "ladder" types ideal for outside a kitchen door. More stylish is a metal French étagère displaying ceramic flowerpots, taking center stage on a patio. Filled with Mediterranean herbs plus a small citrus, geraniums, or a miniature rose, a corner étagère will also make good use of space. Remember to put shade-tolerant parsley and lettuce on lower shelves or move the plants around. A wide flight of steps can be home to edibles, too, especially in a shady space where steps going up might be the only sunny spot. Be aware of tripping hazards and make sure the pots cannot be blown over by wind.

Roof gardens

The increasing interest in edible gardening in cities has refreshed the idea of roof gardens with new lightweight materials. Opt for lightweight containers, such as wood, plastic, or fiberglass, and use a lightweight potting mix, or try hydroponic systems that rely on water, rather than soil. You can also attach plant pouches to screens used for shelter and privacy.

Hanging baskets are a good choice for tumbling cherry tomatoes, keeping them off the ground away from dirt.

Small Bites

This selection of planting ideas is suitable for the smallest containers. Keeping the containers small makes them easy to move around—from outdoor tabletops to decks, from patio corners to border edges. And you can grow your own vegetables and herbs in even the tiniest spaces. Fast-growing leafy crops, such as salad greens and herbs, and single specimens of prolific vegetables, such as chilies and certain types of tomatoes, suit small containers. Adding annual edible flowers, such as marigolds, along with small bedding plants will add color to your vegetable haven.

Salad Bowl

This mixture of salad greens, herbs, and flowers packed into a basket yields a variety of edible treats from early summer to fall, providing a constant supply of fresh lettuce, oregano, and edible petals. The planting is portable—simply pick up the basket and move it to a new position. Keep the basket high up on a table or elsewhere, away from slugs and snails that will be attracted to the lettuce.

You will need

Wire basket with handle,
   8 x 14 inches (20 x 35 cm)

Lining material, such as coir or
   sheet moss (dried sphagnum
   in sheets)

Sheet of plastic 8 x 12 inches
   (20 x 30 cm)

Potting mix

2 lettuce plants

1 oregano plant

2 French marigold plants

Planting your pot

1. Line the basket with the lining material, letting it drape over the edge of the basket. Place a sheet of plastic along the bottom of the basket (to prevent too much water from draining through), then add the potting mix. Trim the lining material to just below the edge of the basket.

2. Plant the basket in spring using young plants. Lettuce and oregano (*Origanum vulgare*) are hardy, but French marigolds are tender, so keep the planting somewhere light and frost free until there is no danger of frost, then harden off and move outside.

3. Keep the potting mix moist, and in hot sunny weather move the basket to partial shade. You can harvest heart-forming lettuce whole, then remove the root and add new young lettuce plants. Or, if growing loose-leaf lettuce, use scissors to cut little and often.

4. Oregano leaves have the best flavor before the plant flowers, but the flowers are edible, too, and they are loved by butterflies and bees. If the plant starts to crowd out the lettuce, cut it back. Deadhead French marigolds often to keep more flowers forming.

 Grow for it!

New ways, old baskets

This container is a copy of a traditional French market basket, made of steel wire mesh with a wooden handle. Its practical design allows for the vegetables to be harvested, then rinsed under running water while they are still in the basket. These strong baskets, if lined, make lightweight and portable containers for salads and herbs. You can keep one on an outdoor table or bench or hang it on a door handle. You may find models with wire lids that can be unclipped with pliers if you want to use them as containers.

Speedy Stir-Fry

Stir-frying is one of the quickest ways to prepare tasty greens, and the ingredients are fast growers, too. You can sow bok choy and other Asian greens in the same container. A terra-cotta bowl, the type often used for small spring bulbs, is just about big enough to provide several servings. In this planting, a white-stemmed bok choy is teamed with red mustard leaf.

You will need

Shallow terra-cotta bowl, with a drainage hole, 12 inches (30 cm) in diameter, 6 inches (15 cm) deep

Drainage material, such as broken clay pot pieces

Potting mix

Packet of mixed Asian greens or separate packets of bok choy and red mustard leaf seeds

Balanced all-purpose fertilizer

Planting your pot

1. Put just a few broken clay pot pieces over the drainage hole, then fill the bowl with potting mix, firm the surface, and sow the seeds 1 inch (2.5 cm) apart.

2. Thin out in stages by removing every other plant for baby leaves and leave about six bok choy plants to grow bigger for cooked greens. Prioritize the boy choy over the red mustard leaf because the latter is very hot and not as useful in the kitchen.

3. Keep the potting mix continually moist so the bok choy grows without a disturbance to its growth and produces succulent stems. Feed with a balanced all-purpose fertilizer every other week to keep the leaves healthy.

4. Bok choy attracts slugs and snails; keeping the bowls on outdoor tables will make it difficult for them to reach. Flea beetles can disfigure leaves; use a fine mesh cover if they are around.

5. Cut alternate bok choy plants off at the stem, leaving room for the others to grow. Snip mustard leaves off as required.

Asian greens stir-fry

In a small mixing bowl, prepare a sauce by whisking together 3 tablespoons soy sauce, 1 tablespoon rice wine winegar, 1 tablespoon oyster sauce, 3 cloves finely chopped garlic, 1 teaspoon crushed red pepper, 1 teaspoon sugar, and ½ teaspoon black ground pepper; set aside. Rinse and dry 6 heads bok choy; if large, cut in half lengthwise. Then heat 1 tablespoon canola oil in a wok or large, heavy skillet set over high heat, add the bok choy, and stir-fry for 1 minute. Pour over the sauce, cover with a lid, and cook over medium heat for about 3 minutes, until tender. Serve as a side dish.

Trio of Chilies

Aficionados of the chili will focus on its shape, color, flavor, and hotness. When growing your own chilies, choose varieties that yield a crop before the end of the growing season in your area. The size of plants varies—this trio represents the range of plant sizes and shapes you might come across, including a Spanish Padron chili.

You will need

Wicker basket, 16 inches (40 cm) in diameter, 12 inches (30 cm) deep

Bushel basket, 10 inches (25 cm) in diameter, 10 inches (25 cm) deep

Wicker basket, 10 inches (25 cm) in diameter, 8 inches (20 cm) deep

Potting mix

1 Padron chili

2 other chili varieties in different sizes, one compact but high yielding, and another upright and early

6 small coriander plants

Tomato fertilizer

Planting your pots

1. Buy a plant of each variety instead of growing from seeds. The plants are frost sensitive, so buy plants in small 4-inch (10-cm)-diameter pots and keep them in a light, frost-free place. Next transfer them into larger pots, and then pinch off the growing tips to keep the plants bushy. Or you can wait until there is no more risk of frost and buy more mature specimens in 8-inch (20-cm)-diameter pots with the growing tips already pinched off.

2. Place mature plants into slightly larger attractive flowerpots. Be sure to make drainage holes, if necessary, so water doesn't sit in the bottom. Grow a compact, spreading plant in its own pot. Add coriander plants around an upright plant. The plants might need staking, depending on the variety and how much of the tips were pinched off earlier.

3. Feed the chili plants with a tomato fertilizer when the first flowers start to appear and supply water during dry spells. When watering spreading plants, direct the water at the potting mix, not the plant. Cut the leaves of the coriander plant, using a pair of scissors, for fresh cilantro leaves as required.

Tapas peppers

Padron peppers, or Pimientos de Padron, were brought to Spain by Mexican monks in the eighteenth century, where they are still grown and served whole in tapas dishes.

Cut 8–10 green chilies from the plant, using pruners and leaving the stem intact. Wash and dry the chilies. Sauté the whole chilies in hot olive oil in a skillet over high heat until the skin is blistered, turning occasionally with tongs. Sprinkle with salt and serve. Eat by holding the stem. The green chilies are sweet but 1 out of 10 is hot, so be prepared for heat.

Mini Moussaka

Eggplants take a while to get going, but as the season progresses they become substantial patio plants with ornamental flowers, followed by colorful edible fruits. For this planting, a silver metal pot was used to house a single eggplant. Ornamental flowers are included to provide more visual interest through the summer, as well as herbs to provide flavor for the long-awaited moussaka.

You will need

Galvanized metal pot, with drainage holes, 15 inches (38 cm) in diameter, 13 inches (33 cm) high

Potting mix

Drainage material, such as broken clay pot pieces or gravel

1 eggplant

1 verbena (trailing type)

1 *Convolvulus sabatius* or 1 oregano plant

3 thyme plants

Tomato fertilizer

Planting your pot

1. Eggplants need a long, warm growing season to fruit, but they are also sensitive to cold. To grow one or two plants, wait until late spring, then buy young started plants. Transfer them to larger pots a couple of times to avoid disturbing root growth and keep them in a bright, warm location. For a bushy plant, pinch off the growing tips when they are 8 inches (20 cm) high.

2. In early summer, they will be ready to be transferred to the final pot. Add drainage material to the bottom of the pot and add the potting mix; metal and lightweight pots need heavier drainage to help prevent the planting from tipping over. Plant the eggplant in the center, at the same level it was in its original pot. Make sure the plant is straight; it will probably need supporting stakes.

3. The space between the plant and the edge of this container is limited. We added two trailing ornamentals for their lavender blooms, but you could use oregano. Thyme fills in neatly around the edge. All these plants like warm, sunny sites and can tolerate dryness at the roots.

4. Water the eggplant well and give it a tomato fertilizer when the first flowers start to form. When they are ready for harvesting, cut off the fruits. Wear gloves if the eggplant variety has spines. Toward the end of the growing season, if the fruits are still developing, move the pot under cover at night.

Bright Lights

This no-nonsense planting is filled with edibles that are easy to grow from seeds or started plants. Each crop is grown in its own pot for maximum yield. The trio offers both young pickings for salad and mature vegetables for cooking. Swiss chard leaves are a spinach substitute, and the stems can be stir-fried. Carrots can be steamed, boiled, or stir-fried, and lettuce can be made into soup.

You will need

1 glazed terra-cotta pot, with drainage holes, 12 inches (30 cm) in diameter, 9 inches (23 cm) deep

1 glazed terra-cotta pot, with drainage holes, 10 inches (25 cm) in diameter, 5 inches (12.5 cm) deep

1 glazed terra-cotta pot, with drainage holes, 9 inches (23 cm) in diameter, 8 inches (20 cm) deep

Drainage material, such as broken clay pot pieces

Potting mix

Swiss chard 'Bright Lights' seeds or transplants

Carrot seeds or seed tape

Lettuce seeds or started plants

Fine mesh cover

Balanced all-purpose fertilizer

Planting your pots

1. Fill each pot with drainage material and potting mix. Firm the surface so you can sow directly into the pots, then cover with a thin layer of potting mix. Alternatively, transplant young started plants into the pots.

2. 'Bright Lights' is the best Swiss chard for containers, because the colorful stems are ornamental, and they are also milder in taste than the red type. Sow seeds in seed-starting trays and transplant them into their final pot once you can identify the colors you want—yellow, pink, and orange are tasty. Use the biggest of the three pots; the roots will eventually fill it. Keep the potting mix moist to prevent the stems from becoming tough.

3. Carrots need their own pot so the seeds can germinate without being disturbed; they also need less water than leafy crops. For long roots, choose deep containers, such as buckets, but for baby or stubby carrots, an 8-inch (20-cm)-deep pot is fine. Scatter the seeds; later on thin to 1 inch (2.5 cm) apart. Lift the pot 3 feet (90 cm) off the ground or use a fine mesh to deter carrot fly.

4. Lettuce roots are shallow so use the smallest pot. In this example, a couple of loose-leaf lettuce have been left to fill the pot and will be harvested all at once. Provide a balanced all-purpose fertilizer, if needed. Keep the soil moist and move to a shaded spot in hot weather to keep the leaves sweet and tender.

Flowers for Salads

Here is a colorful mixture of edible flowers and foliage in a light container, ideal for the edge of a deck, top of a low wall, or a tabletop. The highlight is the mauve spires of African basil contrasting with the orange pompons of the pot marigold, but also waiting in the wings are edible mauve flowers to come from the oregano and chive plants. All the flowers will help beneficial insects, too.

You will need

A fiberglass oval container, 16 inches (40 cm) long, 8 inches (20 cm) at its widest point, and 7 inches (18 cm) deep

Drainage material, such as a few broken clay pot pieces or packing peanuts

Potting mix

2 'African Blue' basils

2 pot marigolds (*Calendula officinalis* 'Porcupine')

1 young oregano plant

2 young chive plants

2 basil plants with colorful leaves, such as purple

2 cinnamon basil plants or other small-leaved basil plants

Planting your pot

1. Fill the container with some drainage material, such as broken clay pot pieces or packing peanuts, then add a potting mix. Keep everything as lightweight as possible so the display can be moved around.

2. When planting an oval shape, start in the middle at the widest point—with the ornamental 'African Blue' basil plants and oregano plant, then work toward the edge. The 'Porcupine' pot marigold was chosen for its brightly colored quilled petals and long flowering period, but any compact variety will do.

3. Fill in the gaps with smaller plants, such as a selection of different basil plants and some young chive plants at each end; the latter will soon produce mauve pompon flowers. The container needs a warm, sunny site and minimal watering because all are drought tolerant.

4. Harvest flowers as required in the morning after the dew has dried. The chives and oregano can be cut back to the base if they get scruffy, and they will produce new leaves. Pot marigolds can get powdery mildew in hot or overcrowded conditions; remove affected leaves. Basil blackens and dies at the first sign of frost; when this happens, it's time to dismantle the planting.

Rally Round Rosemary

Left to its own devices, rosemary is a sprawling shrub, but here it has been trained into an edible topiary and planted in a good-quality flowerpot. The companion plants were chosen because they are neat and low growing, so they will not distract from the shape. This planting makes an attractive front-door display, and a pair on each side of an entrance would add a formal touch.

You will need

Frost-resistant terra-cotta flowerpot, 13 inches (32 cm) in diameter, 12 inches (30 cm) high

Drainage material, such as broken clay pot pieces, gravel, or packing peanuts

Soil-based potting mix

Garden-quality clean sand

1 rosemary plant, already trained as a standard

3 calibrachoa plants

1 variegated lemon thyme plant

Planting your pot

1. Despite the dainty appearance of the top growth, the rosemary's roots are surprisingly big and will take up most of a pot of this size. Add about 2 inches (5 cm) of drainage material to the bottom of the pot, then plant the rosemary at the same level it was in its original pot, using a soil-based potting mix with some sand mixed in (about a handful to every four handfuls of potting mix). Make sure the plant is as straight as possible; if it is young, the plant might need the supporting stake left in place until the main stem stiffens.

2. For summer color, plant the calibrachoa around the edge. These are neat-growing tender annuals with small petunia-like flowers that come in a range of colors, so you can match their color to the flowerpot. You can divide a low-growing thyme and plant the divisions to fill in the gaps under the rosemary stem, but the planting would look equally attractive with a mulch of small gray gravel. Let the potting mix dry out slightly between watering.

3. The rosemary will flower in spring. Afterward you can trim it to shape and use the trimmings in the kitchen. Trim the thyme if it gets straggly.

4. The calibrachoa will die once the first frosts arrive. Remove and replace it with purple violas or more gray gravel. The other plants are evergreen and will survive in many areas during the winter, especially in the shelter of an entrance.

Pick a Pepper

Sweet red peppers are useful in the kitchen, and they look good in the garden, too. In this case, a small variety has been partnered with a bowl-shaped outdoor container. The pot matches the low but spreading shape of the plant, and it is the right shape for a tabletop or low wall. There is still room to squeeze in some young prostrate rosemary and pretty flowers for edging.

You will need

Glazed, bowl-shaped terra-cotta pot, 14 inches (35 cm) in diameter, 7 inches (18 cm) deep

Small square of mesh

Drainage material

Potting mix

1 small sweet red pepper plant

2 small prostrate rosemary plants

2 *Bacopa* species plants or any ornamental trailing plant that matches the container

Tomato fertilizer

Planting your pot

1. If the drainage hole is large and the pot will be on a table, cover the hole with a piece of mesh so the potting mix does not get washed through it, then add drainage material.

2. Fill the pot halfway with potting mix, then tip the sweet pepper plant out of its pot and position it in the center of the container.

3. Position the rosemary and *Bacopa* plants in gaps around the edge of the pot. Fill with the potting mix, making sure there is about 1 inch (2.5 cm) between the top of the pot and the surface of the potting mix for the planting to be watered without the potting mix washing out. Firm the mix in gently. The planting cannot be placed outside until all danger of frost has passed because the sweet pepper is frost sensitive.

4. Supply water during dry spells. When watering the container, avoid soaking any sweet pepper fruits and foliage, because it can cause rotting. Give the sweet pepper a tomato fertilizer when the first flowers start to appear.

5. If foliage is covering the developing fruits, trim it off so the fruits can ripen in the sun. Slugs can eat the fruits, so keep the container off the ground and use copper tape around the outside edge of the container.

6. Cut the rosemary with scissors when needed; cut off the peppers when the skin is red.

Taste of Italy

The smooth line of this stylish planter looks at home in a contemporary setting. Planted with a tomato plant and a circle of sweet basil, the planting is restrained but the ingredients for a future bruschetta are in place. The planter looks like terrazzo, a combination of marble chips and concrete polished until it is smooth—but it is lightweight fiberglass.

You will need

Fiberglass planter, with a terrazzo finish, 14 inches (35 cm) in diameter, 18 inches (45 cm) deep

Drainage material, such as broken clay pot pieces or packing peanuts

Potting mix

Support, such as a garden stake or metal spiral support, plus garden twine

1 indeterminate trained tomato plant

6 sweet basil plants, or 3 sweet basil plants and 2 winter savory

Tomato fertilizer

Planting your pot

1. Add at least one-third drainage material, then potting mix to the container. Plant the tomato plant along with a support, such as a garden stake or metal spiral support.

2. Plant the sweet basil plants around the tomato plant. Both plants are frost sensitive, so wait until there is no danger of frost before hardening off and leaving them outside.

3. Water during dry spells. When watering the container, avoid soaking any sweet basil foliage. Give the tomato plant a tomato fertilizer when the first flowers start to appear. Remove side shoots from the tomato plant to train it upright, and pinch off the tips of the basil plants to encourage plenty of basil foliage. The tomato plant might need tying to the support with garden twine.

4. Harvest the basil leaves as required, and pick the tomatoes when almost ripe, before the skins split.

Bruschetta

Chop 4 tomatoes and put them into a bowl. Tear 4 basil leaves into pieces and add them to the bowl, then pour in 2 tablespoons of olive oil. Add ½ teaspoon salt and ground pepper to taste. Mix and let the flavors combine for a few minutes. Toast 8 slices of Italian bread lightly. Peel a garlic clove and cut it in half, then rub the toasted bread with the cut side. Discard the garlic. Place 2 slices of bread on each plate, and spoon on the tomatoes. Drizzle with a little olive oil and scatter 2 or 3 whole basil leaves over it to garnish.

Lemon Trio

Citrus plants do not have the monopoly on a refreshing lemon flavor. Here three of the best—lemon verbena, lemongrass, and lemon balm—are brought together using a nest of three ceramic flowerpots. This planting will suit a warm patio. Extra white summer flowers have been added for early interest, because the lemongrass and lemon verbena take a while to fill their pots.

You will need

A nest of three ceramic pots, 9, 12, and 16 inches (23, 30, and 40 cm) in diameter

Drainage material, such as broken clay pot pieces

Potting mix

1 lemon verbena (*Aloysia triphylla*)

3 lemongrass (*Cymbopogon citratus*)

1 variegated lemon balm (*Melissa officinalis*)

5 annual chrysanthemums or other daisy-flowered bedding plants, such as marguerites

3 *Bacopa* species plants

Planting your pots

1. Line the bottom of the pot with clay pot pieces and fill with an ordinary potting mix, or use a soil-based mix to keep the plants going year after year.

2. A small leafy lemon verbena bought in spring will grow into a white flowering shrub by summer. In fall, the leaves drop off. You can keep the woody stems frost free in a greenhouse until they sprout the following year. *Bacopa* are low-growing plants, so the lemon verbena's woody framework can develop. The flowers are too small to deadhead, so remove the *Bacopa* when past its best.

3. Lemongrass is a tender grass whose leaves and swollen stem bases are used in Asian dishes. Grow this tropical native as a summer patio plant. Put the plants in the center, then plant around with chrysanthemums.

4. Grow lemon balm on its own in the smallest pot. This perennial can be invasive so growing it in a container is a good way to control it. An alternative for this pot size is a lemon-scented pelargonium, although it is not hardy.

5. Use some of the young leaves immediately, particularly the lemon verbena and lemon balm, because they have more flavor before flowering. At the end of the season, remove the chrysanthemums, then move the containers to a frost-free location if you want to keep the other plantings.

Mint Condition

Capture the refreshing aroma of fresh mint in the smallest of spaces by confining these spreading perennials in flowerpots. Each one of these three flowerpots has a mint with a slightly different flavor: classic spearmint, stronger peppermint, and the milder apple mint or variegated pineapple mint. The pot should be at least 14 inches (35 cm) in diameter, large enough to hold a small mint for a season.

You will need

3 thick terra-cotta pots,
    14 inches (35 cm) in diameter,
    12 inches (30 cm) high

Rich potting mix

1 peppermint (*Mentha × piperita*)

1 spearmint (Tashkent or
    Moroccan mint, *M. spicata*)

1 apple mint or pineapple
    mint (plain or variegated,
    M. suaveolens)

Planting your pots

1. Plant each mint in a container filled with a rich potting mix. Place the finished flowerpots in a sun or partial shade; they will need watering regularly to keep a supply of fresh leaves.

2. Start to pick the leaves as soon as the plants are growing. First pinch off the growing tips for small quantities; later, shear the plant after flowering to stimulate new foliage. The plants flower in summer; these flowers are edible and also attract butterflies and bees.

3. Each year in fall, replant the plants into a larger container with fresh potting mix, because once a plant reaches the edges of its container it starts to deteriorate. Mint can be vulnerable to diseases, such as mildew and rust, if starved or overcrowded; in such cases, dispose of all of the plants and start again with fresh plants.

 Grow for it!

Make more of mint

Mint tea is said to be good for digestion and is often drunk at the end of a meal. Simply add a few sprigs of spearmint or peppermint to hot water and strain it after 5 minutes.

The mints featured here are herbaceous perennials, so they will die down in fall. You can keep some growing in a flowerpot on a kitchen windowsill during the winter, or you can harvest all of the mint, wash it, chop it up, and freeze in ice-cube trays with a few drops of water.

Bigger Servings

By increasing the size of the container, the quantity and range of edible plants you can grow will increase, too. Just imagine being self-sufficient in salad greens and zucchini in the summer, with enough beets to pickle and herbs to dry for the winter. Root, bulb, and tuber crops from carrots, shallots, and potatoes become a possibility when using a deeper container. You can also include some perennial treats, such as roses (try making the rose syrup on page 50), or even create an impressive feature with homegrown lemons.

Flowers for Flavor

The sweet smell of roses, a waft of lavender, and the delicate fragrance of pinks are the essence of summer. Here, together in one pot, are the most evocative. Capture some of their fragrance to use in your cooking by picking buds and petals for use in syrups and sugars. Choose a frost-resistant planter if you want to keep these perennials going, and if your climate permits.

You will need

Frost-resistant ceramic planter, 20 inches (50 cm) in diameter, 12 inches (30 cm) deep

Drainage material, such as broken clay pot pieces

Soil-based potting mix

1 small standard (tree-form) rose with pink or red scented blossoms*

3 English lavenders (Lavendula angustifolia)*

3 scented pinks (Dianthus)*

Rose fertilizer

*Buy organically raised plants, or take your own cuttings of lavender or pinks to grow into mature plants. Alternatively, check when the plants were last treated and with what, so you can allow for at least a couple of weeks before harvesting. Pink and red roses are the best for cooking.

Planting your pot

1. Preparation is the key if you are intending to keep the plants in the container for several years. Place the pot in its final position before planting. Add a generous layer of broken clay pot pieces to help water drain, then fill with a good-quality, soil-based potting mix.

2. Start with the rose, being careful to plant it at the same level it was in the original pot and to center it as vertical as possible. Plant the lavenders and pinks alternately around the rose.

3. The rose will need to be kept moist, but the other plants will cope with drying out between watering. Feed with a rose fertilizer three or four weeks after planting.

4. Harvest the blooms in the morning once the dew has dried. Deadhead faded blooms to keep more flowers coming through the summer. You can use lavender foliage sparingly in cooking.

Rose syrup

For the best results, choose fragrant roses and pick them in the morning. To prepare the roses, shake to remove any insects, then rinse under a fine jet of water. Pull off the petals and place on paper towels. With scissors, cut off the bitter white part at the bottom of each petal. In a saucepan over medium heat, add 1 cup water, 3 cups (600 g) sugar, and 1 cup (20 g) rose petals. Bring to a boil and let boil for 10 minutes, or until thickened into syrup; do not let caramelize. Remove from the heat. Strain through a cheesecloth into a sterilized glass jar, let cool, then refrigerate for up to two weeks. Add the syrup to sparkling water or champagne, or pour over fruit or pound cake.

Backyard Salad Bar

Making and growing your own salad bar will provide you with a steady supply of fresh salad greens. Using three modular boxes makes it easier to sow seeds on a regular basis. Alternatively, use three store-bought planters of a similar size. Sow individual ingredients in rows in the boxes to prevent the vigorous ones from taking over and so you can harvest them separately.

You will need

2 x 6-inch (5 x 15-cm) wooden planks, 40 feet (12 m)

Saw for cutting the planks

Drill for holes and weatherproof screws

Heavy-duty black plastic liner

Heavy-duty staples and stapler

Utility knife

Water-based wood stain

Potting mix

5 packets of seeds: arugula, loose-leaf lettuce, parsley, spinach, mustard, and mizuna (see page 126 for alternatives)

Floating row cover

Balanced all-purpose fertilizer

Planting your pots

1. Adapt the shape of the salad bar to fit your space, building the boxes in a straight line or L shape; the dimensions of 18 x 22 inches (45 x 55 cm) for each box works well. Cut the wood to size and use screws to hold them together at the ends. Line the inside of the salad bar with heavy-duty plastic liners and secure in place with staples, then make some slits in them for drainage holes, using an utility knife. Paint the boxes with a water-based stain.

2. Fill the boxes with potting mix. You can fill the bottom with garden soil or compost, but you need fresh potting mix at the top 4–6 inches (10–15 cm).

3. Sow one box in rows 4 inches (10 cm) apart with ½–¾ inch (1–2 cm) between seeds. Mizuna is often the most vigorous, so sow it at one end; arugula is often fast, so sow it at another end. Sow a box every two to three weeks for a continuous supply.

4. Water to keep the potting mix moist, and watch out for slugs and aphids. Cover with a floating row cover for a few weeks if there are cats around or later if flea beetles nibble holes in the arugula.

5. Cut the plants ¾ inch (2 cm) above the soil, leaving a stump. If fertilized and watered, the stumps regrow in three to four weeks; repeat up to three times.

Strawberry Delight

An early variety of June-bearing strawberries with violas planted underneath will provide a pretty spring flower combination as well as tasty, freshly picked summer strawberries. This planting uses a long but lightweight rectangular planter to accommodate five strawberry plants. Or you can plant a mixture of June-bearing and perpetual strawberries for a longer season of fresh fruit.

You will need

Plastic planter, 30 x 10 x 10 inches (75 x 25 x 25 cm)

Drainage material, such as broken clay pot pieces or gravel

Empty 3-inch (7.5-cm) plastic flowerpot

Soil-based potting mix

5 'Elsanta' (or other early variety, such as 'Earliglow') started strawberry plants in spring

10 violas

Straw (optional)

Tomato fertilizer

Planting your pot

1. Add a drainage layer to the bottom of the planter, using gravel or old broken clay pot pieces. Position an empty flowerpot, right way up, in the middle; you will use it to quickly deliver water to the roots.

2. Add the potting mix, firming it in well—including into the corners—as you fill the container. This will reduce any settling when it is watered, otherwise the plants will sink. Plant the strawberries so the crown of the plant is just above the potting mix surface.

3. Water carefully to avoid wetting the flowers; during heavy rain, provide shelter for the flowers to prevent gray mold from developing, which can infect the flowers and fruit. Start applying a tomato fertilizer once the plants start to flower.

4. As the berries start to ripen, keep them clean by tucking some straw under the fruit near the surface of the potting mix. Pick the berries every day or every other day.

Strawberries and meringue

Rinse 2 cups (225 g) strawberries, remove the stems, and cut in half or quarters, depending on their size. Put the strawberries in a bowl, sprinkle with 1 tablespoon sugar, and stir to mix, crushing a few berries against the sides. Chill. Meanwhile, whip 2 cups (475 ml) heavy whipping cream until it forms soft peaks. Crumble 6 plain meringues into the cream, then mix in the chilled strawberries and stir gently. Pile into individual dessert bowls and serve.

Shady Ladies

Although a sunny site is the most productive for the majority of plants, many people have shady areas in their outdoor space. But as long as these have sun for part of the day or get dappled shade, they can be productive sites, too. This container was started in early spring with tulips, French tarragon, and young lettuce. After flowering, the tulips were removed and replaced with begonias.

You will need

Rectangular wooden planter,
 12 x 15 x 8 inches
 (30 x 38 x 20 cm)

Drill (optional)

Plastic liner

Utility knife

Drainage material, such as
 broken clay pieces or pebbles

Potting mix

1 French tarragon plant

6 tulip plants

2 small red lettuce plants (any
 type, but loose-leaf lettuce
 would be best)

2 begonia plants with red flowers

Planting your pot

1. Drill drainage holes in the planter, if necessary. Next position the liner inside the planter, and cut some slits in the liner for drainage. Add the drainage material and fill the planter with the potting mix.

2. Plant the French tarragon along the back edge of the planter, in the middle, then plant started tulips on either side of it for spring color. Plant young red lettuce plants along the front edge.

3. The planter can be placed at the front of a border; rest it on a paving slab to help preserve the wood from damp earth.

4. After the tulips' flowers have died back, remove the plants, roots and all, and fill the spaces with red begonias. The lettuce and tarragon will grow to fill the space.

5. Harvest the lettuce and tarragon as needed. More young lettuce plants can be added. Keep the potting mix just moist; there is no need to fertilize.

6. At the end of the season, you will still have the tarragon; you can let it continue to grow and fill the container.

 Grow for it!

More shade-tolerant plants

Herbs Chervil, chives, lemon balm, mint

Vegetables Beets, kale, radish, spinach

Flowers Impatiens, nasturtium, violas

Zucchini Feast

The humble zucchini has been given a makeover by choosing a yellow variety and planting it in a feature container along with some bright edible flowers. This copper-blue "Bell Jar" is made of fiberglass and is based on a design by sculptor Bill Harling. It forms the centerpiece within a small herb-growing area, but the planting would work equally well in a lined plastic laundry basket.

You will need

Blue fiberglass flowerpot,
   20 inches (50 cm) in diameter

Drainage material

Potting mix

2 bush yellow zucchini plants

3 nasturtium plants or seeds

2 blue-flowered borage plants

Tomato fertilizer

 Grow for it!

Edible flowers

Borage Slight cucumber flavor but mainly used as a garnish for its pretty flowers.

Nasturtium The pepper-flavored flowers add color to salads, rice, and pasta dishes.

Zucchini Used to hold a soft stuffing that is spooned in or dipped in batter and fried.

Planting your pot

1. You can raise the flowerpot on bricks so it emerges from the surrounding plants. Fill the bottom one-third to one-half of the pot with drainage material or a mixture of drainage material and garden soil, then add fresh potting mix.

2. Make a slight mound in the center of the pot. When there is no danger of frost, plant two hardened-off zucchini plants in the center. Let the plants become established, being careful to water the surrounding soil, not the stems or foliage.

3. Arrange the nasturtium plants around the rim or insert seeds into the surface. Choose a cultivar with variegated foliage as well as a range of orange and red flowers.

4. Once the other plants are well-established, insert the borage to fill any gaps. All three plants have edible flowers and attract beneficial insects.

5. As the zucchini form, remove any shriveled blooms. Apply a tomato fertilizer and increase watering. Cut back the nasturtiums and borage if they start to look straggly.

Pasta with zucchini

Cook 1 pound (450 g) of tagliatelle or fettuccini according to package directions. Reserve and set aside ½ cup cooking liquid. Meanwhile, heat 2 tablespoons olive oil in a saucepan over medium-high heat. Add 1 thinly sliced shallot and sauté for 2–3 minutes, stirring often. Add 2 zucchini cut into cubes and sauté for 3–4 minutes. Add the pasta to the saucepan, along with half the reserved cooking liquid, toss to coat the noodles, and cook for 1–2 minutes. Season to taste with salt and ground black pepper, turn off the heat, and stir in ¼ cup (175 g) crumbled goat cheese and grated zest from a lemon.

Pick of the Day

From this one container, you will have a long season of regular pickings that will provide you with fresh, flavorsome herbs through the seasons and a summer salad of lettuce and tomatoes. By using a square container, you can space the plantings in three "rows," packing in a surprising amount. The planting contains a mixture of hardy and tender subjects, with some perennials and some annuals.

You will need

Square fiberglass planter, 16 x 16 x 16 inches (40 x 40 x 40 cm)

Drainage material, such as broken clay pot pieces, gravel, or packing peanuts

Multipurpose potting mix

1 small cherry tomato plant

1 dwarf lavender plant

1 purple-leaved basil plant

4 small green loose-leaf lettuce

1 chive plant

1 oregano plant

Tomato fertilizer

Planting your pot

1. Put in about 2 inches (5 cm) of drainage material, then add the potting mix, pushing plenty of potting mix into each corner.

2. Start with the tomato, because depending on its size, you may need to adjust the number and position of the other plants. Plant it into one corner; it may need up to one-quarter of the planter. Plant the other corners with the lavender, basil, oregano, and chives. If the clump of chives is large, divide it into smaller sections.

3. Now fill in the gaps with small lettuce, perhaps three in the middle row and one between the tomato and basil. Keep spare plants in separate pots for replacements later on.

4. First cut the chive and oregano foliage; they are tasty when they are young and it keeps the plants small. Pick the lavender flowers when in bud. Cut the loose-leaf lettuce as you need it. Later, the chives and oregano will flower; you can eat the petals.

5. When flowering, start to fertilize the tomato plant. Pick ripe tomatoes and the basil. Remove the lettuce when it begins to set seeds in the summer. In the fall, remove the tomato and basil.

 Grow for it!

Alternative colors

Each of the six subjects in the recipe has alternatives in different colors, so there are many color combinations. Cherry tomatoes are also available with yellow or orange fruit, which can be paired with a red-leaved lettuce and a green-leaved Genovese basil. A speciality herb nursery can supply, for example, white-flowered chives, golden oregano, and a paler mauve lavender.

Bouquet Garni Box

A bouquet garni is a small bundle of different herbs tied together or tied inside a cheesecloth bag and added to slow-cooking meat dishes and stews. The herbs in this planting provide more than enough leaves for the traditional bouquet garni of bay leaf, parsley, and thyme. And there are other herbs to make it a complete cook's package: sage (for pork), rosemary (for lamb), and tarragon (for poultry and fish).

You will need

1 recycled packing crate, 14 x 21 inches (36 x 53 cm), 10 inches (25 cm) deep

Two 2-foot (60-cm) burlap squares

18 x 25-inch (45 x 64-cm) piece of black flexible pond liner from an aquatic store

Utility knife

Drainage material, such as broken clay pot pieces or packing peanuts

Potting mix with perlite mixed in

1 small bay tree (*Laurus nobilis*)

1 prostrate rosemary plant

1 flat-leaf parsley plant

1 French tarragon plant

1 sage plant

1 golden-leaved thyme plant

1 silver-leaved thyme plant

Planting your pot

1. Line the crate with the burlap, then cover the bottom with the pond liner, letting it extend an inch or two up the sides. Make some drainage slits into the pond liner. Add a 2-inch (5-cm) layer of a lightweight drainage material.

2. Woody herbs grow better in a soil-based potting mix, but to keep this planting portable, use a lightweight potting mix with perlite added for drainage. The bay tree is the most valuable and you can replant it in its own container of soil-based potting mix at the end of the season and move it indoors for winter.

3. Position the bay tree in the center and pack potting mix around it. Space out the other herbs, with three at the back and three at the front. We have used large pots of herbs for instant cover, but you can use smaller pots and mulch the spaces in between with gravel.

4. There are plenty of herbs to provide fresh leaves from spring to fall. Because woody herbs with tough leaves (bay, sage, rosemary, and thyme) dry well (see "Drying herbs," right), preserve them at their peak in midsummer.

Drying herbs

A microwave oven speeds up the drying process. Harvest the leaves before the plant flowers and in the morning after the dew has dried. Clean the leaves, removing any discolored, dirty, or diseased ones. Lay them out on a single layer of two sheets of paper towel. Microwave for 2 minutes, check and, if not dry, microwave again for 30 seconds. Use clean, dry hands to crumble the leaves into clean, dry screw-top jars labeled with the herb and date. Bay leaves are best in a wide-neck jar and stored whole, not crumbled.

Sweet Sisters

Here's a modern recipe inspired by the traditional "three sisters" planting of corn, beans, and squash practiced by Native Americans. Corn makes an impressive foliage feature, but here we used sweet potato instead of squash because sweet potato tubers require less space in the pot. A plastic container is ideal because it is large, yet light enough to be moved around and to tip out the tubers.

You will need

Heavy-duty plastic planter, 18 inches (45 cm) in diameter, 16 inches (40 cm) deep

Drill for holes

Drainage material, such as a few broken clay pot pieces or packing peanuts

Potting mix

5 corn seeds

4 bush bean seeds (or 4 small sweet pepper plants)

1 started sweet potato plant

5 small nasturtium plants or seeds

Tomato fertilizer (if growing pepper plants)

Planting your pot

1. You need a pot that is deep and can hold at least five corn plants (to improve pollination). Make drainage holes in the pot. Fill the bottom with a drainage layer. Add the potting mix, mounding it in the center and firming down gently.

2. All the vegetables are tender and cannot be planted outside until after the last frost. Start the beans and corn in individual peat pots in a light, frost-free place in spring; buy a young sweet potato plant.

3. Plant the sweet potato in the center of the mound, plant the corn around it, then add the beans or peppers. Finally, add the nasturtiums at the edge of the planter as either started plants or seeds. Keep the container in a warm, sheltered place; the corn may need support. Apply organic slug pellets.

4. The nasturtiums add early color and some edible flowers; remove them later on if they get too straggly in hot weather. When the bush beans start to crop, pick the beans regularly for a steady supply. If you are growing sweet peppers, they will appear later and will benefit from a tomato fertilizer.

5. Harvest the cobs when the silks start to turn brown and remove the corn plants when depleted. Tip out and harvest the sweet potatoes 100–110 days after planting. The tubers will be small, so they won't store well for long.

Flavors to Savor

From this one pot you will have refreshing anise seed leaf bases and foliage, celery-flavored stems and leaves for soups or stock, and hot, spicy salad greens. All need a moist, rich soil, so a large, thick terra-cotta flowerpot was used to hold plenty of potting mix. The green foliage and terra-cotta pot forms a calm backdrop in the yard, and there are plenty of flavors for the cook.

You will need

Terra-cotta flowerpot,
    18 inches (45 cm) in diameter,
    12 inches (30 cm) deep

Heavy-duty plastic liner and
    utility knife (depending on
    choice of flowerpot)

Drainage material, such as
    broken clay pot pieces

Rich potting mix

3 celery plants

3 Florence fennel plants

3 upland cress seedlings
    (or use watercress, see
    "Watercress," right)

Balanced all-purpose fertilizer

Planting your pot

1. The flowerpot should be thick and heavy, so place it in its final location before filling with the drainage material and a moisture-retentive, rich potting mix. If you use a terra-cotta flowerpot with thinner sides, first line it with heavy-duty black plastic and cut some slits in it at the bottom for drainage holes.

2. Start by positioning the young fennel plants in the center of the pot, then add the young celery plants and finish with some upland cress or watercress seedlings.

3. Check the container daily and, if needed, water to keep the potting mix moist. The celery, in particular, needs fertilizing with a balanced all-purpose fertilizer within a few weeks of planting and every few weeks afterward.

4. The upland cress will be ready first in early summer; cut with scissors as required. The Florence fennel will form small swollen leaf bases by the end of the summer. Cut these off at the bottom; leave the roots, which will grow some more foliage that can then be used as you would herb fennel. The celery will produce thin stems, which will be slightly blanched by the upland cress.

 Grow for it!

Watercress

You can sow watercress from seeds in the spring or take a cutting from a bunch of watercress and root it in a small pot of potting mix. Keep it damp until it is growing well, then plant outside into the final container. Keep it watered and fertilized. Remove any flowers and cut leaves as you need them.

Citrus Sense

A citrus plant, with its heady, scented flowers and juicy fruit, will give a patio a Mediterranean feeling, especially if you use a Versailles-style planter. It is named after a type of wooden box used at Versailles Palace in France for plants that spent summer on the terrace and winter inside. Lemons are practical for small yards in warm climates; even a small plant 3 feet (90 cm) tall will yield a large number of fruit.

You will need

Wooden Versailles planter,
  12 x 15 x 15 inches
  (30 x 38 x 38 cm)

Heavy-duty liner

Utility knife

Citrus potting mix (or a soil-
  based mix with added sand to
  improve drainage)

1 grafted lemon tree *(Citrus limon)*

4 lemon variegated thyme plants

Citrus fertilizer

Planting your pot

1. Position the liner (usually supplied with the planter) and make some drainage holes in it. Add some citrus potting mix, usually available from an online source.

2. Select a lemon tree with fruit already forming; the fruit will grow and ripen slowly but will hang on the tree until you are ready to use them. Remove the plant from its original pot, put it carefully in the center of the planter, and fill it with potting mix. Any underplanting needs to be drought tolerant and discrete, such as thyme; plant one in each corner.

3. Place the planter in a light, sheltered position. Let the mix dry out a little between watering. Feed with a citrus fertilizer, following the manufacturer's directions. Thin out fruitlets so there is only one fruit per cluster. Trim the thyme if it gets straggly.

4. Citrus can sit outside from early summer to early fall (June to September) but it needs to overwinter in a sunroom or elsewhere with a minimum temperature of 45°F (7°C). Potted citrus plants are heavy; to move one, use a plant trolley or use a planter supplied with wheels.

Preserved lemons

Use the juice from preserved lemons to flavor salad dressings, soups, and meat, fish, or chicken sauces. Quarter 5 lemons almost to the bottom, sprinkle salt on the exposed flesh, and reshape the fruit. Pack the lemons into a sterilized jar in layers with ¼ cup (55 g) salt, 1 tablespoon olive oil, 1 cinnamon stick, 3 cloves, 4 black peppercorns, 6 coriander seeds, and 2 bay leaves between the layers. Press the lemons to release their juices, adding freshly squeezed lemon juice to cover them. Seal the jar, and keep it in a warm place for 30 days, shaking the jar every day. They will keep for 6 months; refrigerate after opening.

Fire Pit

A kadai is an Indian circular, metal pot used over a fire to cook for large get-togethers, such as weddings and festivals. Recycled kadai may be imported and used outside on low stands as barbecues or plant holders. This kadai has been planted with an impromptu display of edibles in a vibrant display of yellow, purple, orange, and red.

You will need

Recycled kadai (available online, or an old, shallow metal container), 32 inches (80 cm) in diameter

Plastic liner or newspaper

3 yellow sweet pepper plants, with supporting stakes or a few dowels

2 large pots of purple-flowered thyme plants

2 large pots of chive plants

2 large pots of parsley plants

2 large pots of coriander plants

Packing material, such as newspaper or packing peanuts (optional)

Potting mix

12 pots of nasturtium plants

Drainage material, such as packing peanuts (optional)

Planting your pot

1. For a temporary display to act as a centerpiece, line the container with plastic or newspapers to protect the surface. Water all the plants well beforehand. Place the pots of sweet peppers in the center—look for ones with supporting stakes in place or add your own by using dowels.

2. Set out the herbs in a circle around the sweet peppers; you can leave them in their pots and raise the height up with newspaper or packing peanuts. Finish off with a layer of potting mix to hide the packing materials.

3. Set out the nasturtiums in pots around the edge and cover with potting mix. You can plan ahead and grow these from seeds by planting them into small flowerpots in early spring.

4. The plants will last for a couple of days without watering. By then, you will need to water directly into the pots.

5. If you want a more permanent display, add drainage material to the bottom of the kadai before adding some potting mix, then remove the plants from their pots before planting and firm around them with potting mix. You may want to remove the nasturtiums once they fade in hot weather.

Crops in Corners

Square planters add a formal touch and are versatile. They are also ideal for making the most use of space in corners. Plus they are beautiful as centerpieces on their own or set out with similar planters to form an edge to a patio area. In this case, a large pepper plant takes center stage, with a small cherry tomato plant, foliage herbs, and summer bedding positioned underneath to create a vibrant planting.

You will need

Fiberglass planter, 13 inches (33 cm) square and deep

Drill for making drainage holes

Drainage material, such as broken clay pot pieces, gravel, or packing peanuts

Potting mix

1 pepper plant, either sweet or hot

2 calibrachoa plants

1 small cherry tomato plant

1 flat-leaf parsley plant

1 lemon-scented thyme plant

Tomato fertilizer

Planting your pot

1. Make drainage holes in the planter, then add plenty of drainage material and potting mix. Make sure you push plenty of potting mix into each corner.

2. The pepper, tomato, and bedding plants are frost sensitive, so do not plant outside until all danger of frost has passed and the plants have been hardened off.

3. Start with the pepper plant; depending on its size, you may need to adjust the number and position of the other plants. Plant the pepper off center into a corner, then plant a calibrachoa on each side, with the plants cascading out. Next plant the tomato and herbs.

4. The pepper and tomato plants may need supporting stakes. Place in a warm, sunny spot. Start cutting the herb foliage first; the leaves are more tasty when young and it keeps the plants producing leaves. Feed with a tomato fertilizer to promote fruiting on the tomatoes and pepper as well as flowers on the calibrachoa. Pick the tomatoes and peppers when ripe.

No-cook mixed pickle

It is easy to pickle firm-textured vegetables, such as cauliflower, cucumbers, green beans, pearl onions, and peppers. Prepare the vegetables as you would for a recipe, trimming and cutting them into florets, slices, or wedges. Soak them for 1–2 days in 1½ cups (450 g) salt mixed with 20 cups (4.5 liters) water. Drain the vegetables, rinse, and dry thoroughly. Pack the vegetables in a sterilized, airtight container, leaving a 1-inch (2.5-cm) gap at the top; cover completely with a herb or spice vinegar, mixed with sugar to taste. Place a wax paper circle and plastic wrap on top to seal, then tightly secure the lid. Store in the refrigerator for up to three months.

Patriotic Potatoes

Growing your own potatoes in pots or bags is popular because you don't need a vegetable garden, and it avoids diseases that can be picked up from garden soil. It is a fun project to do with children. Here are heirloom varieties to provide a mixture of red, white, and blue potatoes, but you can, of course, use any potato variety.

You will need

1 terra-cotta flowerpot, 20 inches (50 cm) in diameter, 18 inches (45 cm) deep

Drainage material, such as gravel or packing peanuts

Rich potting mix

3 sprouted seed potatoes (see Potatoes, pages 132–33), one each of a red-, white-, and blue-flesh variety

Floating row cover

Balanced all-purpose fertilizer

Planting your pot

1. In mild areas, or if you have a light and frost-free greenhouse or porch, start planting the pot in early spring (March). If you cannot guarantee the plants will be frost free, wait until mid- to late spring (April or May). Prepare your containers. Line the bottom with a layer of gravel or packing peanuts to help drainage. Fill the containers halfway with potting mix.

2. Plant the sprouted seed potatoes and cover with potting mix. As the plants grow, add more potting mix to just cover the growing tips. If frost is in the forecast, cover the container with a floating row cover or bring it indoors.

3. Keep the potting mix moist, but not too wet or the potatoes will rot. Keep adding potting mix until it almost reaches the rim of the container. Water regularly and apply a balanced all-purpose fertilizer every few weeks.

4. When the plants start to bloom, the tubers will be forming. When there are plenty of flowers, push your hand into the potting mix and feel for tubers. If several are the size of a hen's egg, pull them out; leave the plants to produce more. When the top dies down, turn out the potting mix and collect the tubers.

Going UP!

Vertical gardening is all about finding opportunities to grow edibles using the space above. Conventional containers can be turned into havens for vegetables, with window boxes becoming fresh salad bars and hanging baskets making a home for tomatoes. You can transform bare walls and fences into productive areas, thanks to planting pouches or pockets that are ideal for planting with a selection of different crops. Last but not least, there is nothing like climbing beans to fill vertical space productively, so if you have a house, garage, or shed wall facing the sun, put up a trellis or netting and get growing!

Sunshine in a Box

Sunflowers bring a smile to everyone, and they brighten up a windowsill in the front yard. Using a neutral wooden window box lets you decorate or customize the planting. The harvest from the beans will be modest, but their flowers will add a splash of color; make sure you add some herbs to the planter as an edging. The dried sunflower heads are a natural food for birds.

You will need

Wooden window box,
   24 x 10 x 8 inches
   (60 x 25 x 20 cm)

Drill for drainage holes, if
   necessary, and for fittings

Plastic liner

Utility knife

Potting mix

1–3 dwarf sunflower plants

6–8 compact, purple pole
   bean plants

4 small, yellow-variegated
   thyme plants

Support fittings, such as
   screws or brackets

Balanced all-purpose fertilizer

Planting your pot

1. Drill drainage holes into the window box, if necessary. Next position the liner and cut some slits in it for drainage (but first see Step 5 below). Fill the window box with the potting mix.

2. Plant the sunflower in the center of the box—choose a dwarf variety that will do better in a confined space. The sunflower will need regular watering and fertilizing, so you might want a few replacements on hand.

3. Plant the bean plants on either side of the sunflower. Although you are planting a small variety, the plants may still need a little support in windy locations. Plant the beans close together so they will support themselves, but you can also insert some short stakes or branched brush.

4. Fill in the front edge with a low-growing herb, such as thyme; this yellow-variegated thyme picks up the sunflower's yellow petals, and when it blooms, it will have small mauve flowers.

5. Lift the box into position and fasten it. The fittings you use will depend on the type of windowsill and window box. You can hold the box in place by drilling through it and attaching it to the sill with screws. In this case, do so before planting the box; use a stiff liner so you can plant into it, then put it in place.

Stepping Out with Basil

Basil delivers a heady aroma and a taste of the Mediterranean in a neat package. Besides the traditional green-leaved basil, there are varieties with smaller or colorful leaves, ornamental flowers, and spicy flavors. Here are the best of each to make the perfect herbal treat for an urban dweller. Basil doesn't cope with cold, damp, and root disturbance, so buy started plants.

You will need

3 lime-green metal containers,
   6 inches (15 cm) in diameter

1 basil 'Sweet Genovese'

1 basil 'Aristotle'

1 purple-leaved basil plant

Balanced all-purpose fertilizer

* The plants pictured here are on a fire escape, but please note, in practice, they should not be left unsecured on steps, where they could fall off. And they should not block an emergency exit.

Planting your pots

1. Use started plants in 5-inch (13-cm)-diameter pots that fit in the metal containers. For basil sold in 3½-inch (9-cm) pots, you can transfer them into a 5-inch (13-cm) pot and pinch off the plants' growing tips to encourage bushiness, or use two plants per 5-inch (13-cm) pot.

2. Put each potted plant into a metal container; these do not have drainage holes, so you need to lift out the inner pot daily and pour out any water at the bottom of the metal container. You can also place basil on a windowsill, indoors, or outside.

3. The plants need some watering, and if you harvest large-leaved types heavily, apply a balanced all-purpose fertilizer.

4. 'Sweet Genovese' is the one to pick and eat for the classic flavor. 'Aristotle' has small leaves and is neat; trim with scissors to use as a pretty garnish. You can use basil with colorful leaves for cooking, but they are also ornamental, especially when the lilac flowers appear.

Aromatic roasted tomatoes

Preheat the oven to 375°F (190°C). Grease an ovenproof dish with 1 tablespoon of olive oil. Core 2 pounds (900 g) tomatoes, then cut into wedges. Put the tomatoes, cut side up, in the dish. Break up 1 head of garlic into cloves and scatter around the tomatoes. Cut 6 sprigs basil and tuck between the tomatoes, then sprinkle with salt and ground black pepper. Drizzle 2 tablespoons olive oil over the tomatoes. Roast for 30 minutes, until the tomatoes are lightly charred on the outside. Sprinkle with 2 tablespoons freshly torn basil leaves and serve.

Salsa Box

Just as there are many recipes for salsa, this planting is equally flexible, depending on how "hot" you like flavors. The main two plants are a tomato and a pepper. Look for compact varieties suitable for a small pot, then choose a sweet pepper or chili. The 'African Blue' basil looks great in flower, but if you can't find one, any small green basil, coriander, or thyme will work, too.

You will need

Wooden or plastic window box, 24 inches (60 cm) long, 6 inches (15 cm) wide and deep

Drill for drainage holes and for securing the bracket

Bracket fitting and screws for a wooden balcony

Water-based stain (optional)

Liner, stiff or flexible

Drainage material, such as broken clay pieces or gravel

Potting mix

1 dwarf red pepper plant (sweet pepper or chili)

1 tomato plant (tumbler type with medium fruit)

1 ornamental basil 'African Blue'

2 small-leaved basil plants

2 lemon thyme plants or coriander plants

Tomato fertilizer

Planting your pot

1. All the plants are tender, so keep them in a light, frost-free place and harden off well. The advantage of planting into a stiff liner is you can have another liner with a spring planting in the box, then swap them over in early summer when this planting will be ready.

2. Add drainage holes to the box, and apply a water-based stain if needed. Secure the box and bracket to the balcony. Put the plants into a stiff liner and put the liner into the box; alternatively, position the liner before adding the plants. In either case, first add a layer of drainage material and potting mix before adding the plants.

3. Position the pepper at one end of the box and the tomato at the other end; add the basil near the tomato to add height. Fill any gaps with small green herbs. If the box will be viewed from all sides, take this into account when planting.

4. Keep the potting mix moist, and give the pepper and tomato plants a tomato fertilizer to encourage a productive crop.

Salsa

Cut 4 small tomatoes in half widthwise, squeeze out the seeds, and dice. Put them into a bowl with 1 finely chopped clove garlic, 1 seeded and diced sweet red pepper, the juice of half a lime, ½ teaspoon salt, and 1 teaspoon thyme leaves. Stir to blend. For a hot salsa, add 1 small hot chili, seeded and finely chopped. Stir again, then cover and let the flavors blend together for at least 30 minutes before serving.

Goldfinger's Bean Basket

These bush bean plants are prolific croppers and perfect for containers that are lifted off the ground. Unlike when these plants are grown in the ground, the beans will not be splashed with mud, and they will be easier to pick. This well-prepared hanging basket is filled with eye-catching yellow beans, and there is extra color from fresh frilly-leaved red lettuce.

You will need

Hanging basket, with open sides, 14 inches (35 cm) in diameter

Loose liner

Piece of plastic sheet for lining bottom of the basket

Potting mix

Water-retaining granules (in dry regions)

5–6 bush bean plants, any yellow pod variety

3 red loose-leaf lettuce plants

Bracket and screws

Floating row cover

Pruners

Planting your pot

1. Line the bottom of the basket with a loose basket liner, then put in a piece of plastic, working up from the bottom of the basket.

2. Use a potting mix that has water-retaining granules already in the mix, or sprinkle on the granules as directed on the packaging and mix in well. Fill the basket halfway with potting mix.

3. Insert three small bean plants around the sides of the basket, then fill it up with potting mix, firming down gently around the roots. Young, small plants are easier to handle than bigger plants, but handle carefully because beans dislike being transplanted. Plant the top of the basket with the remaining two or three bean plants, plus three small lettuce plants.

4. The bean plants will be sensitive to frost, so be aware of the last frost dates and make sure plants are hardened off well. Protect the plants with a floating row cover, if necessary. Hang the basket in a sunny, sheltered position. Avoid a windy site. Check the basket daily to make sure the potting mix is moist.

5. Harvest the lettuce little and often. Cut off the beans with pruners instead of pulling them; tugging on the beans can dislodge the plant. Pick the beans little and often to encourage more beans to form.

Pick and Mix

This vertical planter with planting pockets is easy to fill and will provide a variety of herbs for cooking. Position it outside the kitchen door on a sunny surface. Almost any edible plant sold in small pots can be used, but we chose long-lasting foliage herbs. To get the horizontal striped effect, keep the same plant type in each row, and vary the colors and textures between rows.

You will need

1 planting pouch, with separate planting pockets arranged in pairs

Fastenings (wall anchors and galvanized screws)

Drill or screwdriver for securing the fastenings

Potting mix

2-4 winter savory or prostrate rosemary plants

2-4 curly parsley plants

2-4 variegated sage plants

2-4 yellow pansies or violas*

* If you want these as edible plants, ask the supplier if they have been sprayed with chemicals. Or grow your own organically from seeds.

Planting your pot

1. Attach the planter to the wall as directed on the package instructions. Choose a height that is convenient for you to water and harvest, but also take into account how much light there is for plant growth.

2. Plants in small 3-inch (7.5-cm)-diameter pots are the easiest to use for this type of planter. Water the plants well before planting. You can use one plant per pocket, adding in extra potting mix and allowing room for the plant to fill out. Or to provide an instant finished look, plant two plants per pocket, adding as much potting mix as you can.

3. When adding extra potting mix, take the time to fill corners. However, leave a gap at the top so when the pockets are watered, the potting mix is not washed out. Water the potting mix so it is barely moist. Start harvesting as soon as the plants are well established.

4. Because each type of plant has its own root area, it is easy to replant any replacements without disturbing other plants.

 ### Grow for it!

Planting pouches

Pouches and other similar planters, where plants are inserted through slits in fabric or plastic, are easier to plant with small started plants. For the best results, keep the pouch or planter lying flat for one or two weeks, so the roots can get established, then hang it up in place. This prevents water from dislodging the young plants.

Sunny Window Box

There are flavors a plenty in this small window box, yet it is decorative, too. The purple foliage is balanced by the softer green of the tarragon and thymes. Many of the herbs can be left to flower or pinched off and trimmed so there are more leaves to harvest. The planting needs a warm sunny spot. However, it is drought-tolerant, apart from the purple shiso, which wilts rapidly but does recover.

You will need

Wooden window box, 24 inches (60 cm) long, 8 inches (20 cm) wide, and 9 inches (23 cm) deep

Drill for drainage holes and securing the bracket

Bracket and screws for a wooden balcony

Liner (flexible)

Utility knife

Drainage material, such as broken clay pieces, gravel, or packing peanuts

Potting mix

1 purple shiso (also known as perilla or Japanese basil; *Perilla frutescens purpurascens*)

1 French tarragon plant

1 purple basil plant

3 basil plants

4 thyme plants

Planting your pot

1. Drill drainage holes in the bottom of the box, and secure the box and bracket to the balcony or fence. Put in the flexible liner, make some drainage slits, and fill with the drainage material, followed by the potting mix.

2. Put the tallest plant (in this case the purple shiso) in the center of the box. Select the next two tallest plants, a basil and tarragon, and plant one at each end of the box.

3. Fill any remaining gaps with the remaining plants. Gaps at the back of the planter can be filled with a basil with flower spikes. The purple basil can be placed in front of the taller basils and one of the thymes at the other end of the box in front of the tarragon. Small plants of thyme form a neat edge under the purple shiso. Firm the plants in well, being careful to push plenty of potting mix into the corners of the box.

4. Pick and use the leaves as required, leaving the basil to provide the flowers. The planting will need watering but not fertilizing.

Tarragon vinegar

Capture the subtle flavor of tarragon by making a vinegar to add to salad dressings, fish, or chicken. Open a 16-ounce (500-ml) screw-top bottle of white wine vinegar, pour off some of the vinegar, then push in a few sprigs of young tarragon leaves and stem. Fill with vinegar, replace the lid, and shake. Within a month, the vinegar will have a subtle flavor. Or, for a stronger flavor, strip off a handful of leaves from their stems. Put in a clean, dry, empty jar. Cover with white wine vinegar, replace the lid, and shake. After a month, strain the vinegar and return it, minus the leaves, to the jar. Remember to label it.

Tomato Catch-Up

Here is a quick-and-easy way to plant and grow tomatoes and herbs. All the ingredients can be bought as young plants in early summer and planted into the top of the basket. A 14-inch (35-cm)-diameter basket provides enough potting mix for the plants, and it needs less regular watering than a smaller basket. The herbs can be varied, but look for low-growing varieties.

You will need

Hanging basket, with open sides, 14 inches (35 cm) in diameter

Coco fiber liner for 14-inch (35-cm) basket

Plastic saucer or piece of flexible plastic

Potting mix

Water-retaining granules (in dry regions)

1 tumbler-type tomato plant

1 compact oregano plant

2 curly parsley plants

1 winter savory plant

1 prostrate rosemary plant

Bracket for a 14-inch (35-cm) basket and screws

Drill or screwdriver for securing the bracket

Tomato fertilizer

Planting your pot

1. Insert the liner into the bottom of the basket, then put it on a saucer or piece of plastic to help retain moisture.

2. Use a potting mix that has water-retaining granules already in the mix or sprinkle in the granules as directed on the package and mix it in well. Fill the basket two-thirds full with potting mix, firming gently as you fill.

3. Plant the tomato plant at the top of the basket, making sure it is in the center, and firm down gently. Continue to pack potting mix around the roots; the plant should be at the same depth that it was in the original pot. Leave a 1-inch (2.5-cm) gap between the top of the mix and the top of the basket.

4. Retain any small supports that came with the tomato plant to help lift the stems above the potting mix. Position the small herb plants around the rim of the basket and firm in gently. The herbs are hardy but the tomato is frost-sensitive, so wait until after the last frost and harden off well before hanging up on a bracket positioned outside in a sunny and sheltered site.

5. Check the basket daily to make sure the potting mix is moist, and use a tomato fertilizer as directed on the package; feeding starts four weeks after planting and then weekly or biweekly thereafter.

Windowsill Pesto

Who would guess this elegant green-and-white summer planting could also provide enough basil for a quick homemade pesto? There are four different herbs within this small window box, but it is the white cascading petunias that catch the eye. The planting area is small so, if possible, make a pair of these window boxes to increase your harvest or adjust quantities to fit a larger box.

You will need

Faux lead window box (fiberglass), 24 inches (60 cm) long, 8 inches (20 cm) wide and deep

Drill for drainage holes (optional)

Drainage material, such as broken clay pieces, gravel, or packing peanuts

Potting mix

4–5 sweet or Genovese basil plants

2 basil plants with large, textured leaves

2 garlic chive plants

1 oregano plant

2 white trailing petunia plants

Planting your pot

1. Make drainage holes in the box if there are none, put in the drainage material, and fill with potting mix.

2. This window box is narrow, so look for young herbs in small pots or raise them yourself from seeds.

3. Position the plants before planting; it will be easier to start with the petunias at each end and then fill in with the smaller plants. Plant the oregano centered along the back edge, with a garlic chive on either side, and fill in with large-leaved basil. Plant the sweet basil in front.

4. The petunia and basil are tender; keep them in a light, frost-free place and harden off well.

5. Keep the potting mix barely moist. Start picking the oregano and chive leaves first, then pick the basil once the plants are growing well. If left alone, all will flower. To keep the planting looking its best, cut the garlic chive leaves down to the base instead of snipping the ends.

Quick pesto

Toast ½ cup (65 g) pine nuts in a dry skillet over medium-high heat, stirring often, for a few minutes until golden. Be careful to avoid letting them burn. Let cool. Add them to the bowl of a food processor with 1 garlic clove, 2 cups (50 g) loosely packed basil leaves, and ½ cup (45 g) grated Parmesan cheese. Chop in bursts until the leaves are shredded, then gradually pour in ¼ cup olive oil with the motor running. It should be thick and smooth. If it looks too dry, stir in a little more olive oil. Taste and add salt and ground black pepper, if necessary.

Pole Position

A sunny surface, such as the back of a fence, garage, or shed, just needs a support and a deep container. You will then be set to grow productive, yet attractive pole beans. To keep the planter looking neat, there is a row of a small-leaved, compact basil forming an edible topiary, which can be clipped into shape as you harvest them. At each end of the planter, a touch of color comes from bright red begonias.

You will need

Plastic planter, 28 inches (70 cm) long, 12 inches (30 cm) wide and deep

Drill for making drainage holes (optional)

Wooden trellis or bean netting, 6 feet (2 m) high, 28 inches (70 cm) wide

Galvanized screws and drill **or** screwdriver to secure the support

Drainage material, such as gravel **or** packing peanuts

Rich potting mix

7 young started pole bean plants

6 young started begonia plants with red flowers

10 young started small-leaved, compact basil plants

Soft garden twine or plant ties

Planting your pot

1. Drill drainage holes in the planter, if necessary. Check the position of the planter, then attach the support, such as a trellis, into place. Position the planter underneath the support and add a layer of drainage material. You can enrich the potting mix by mixing in well-rotted organic matter, such as garden compost.

2. All the plants are frost sensitive so they cannot be planted in the final container until there is no danger of frost (early summer), and they have been completely hardened off.

3. Bean plants don't like disturbance, so handle them carefully. Line the bean plants along the back of the planter, spacing the plants 4 inches (10 cm) apart. Young plants need help to cling to the support, so tie them in using soft garden twine— eventually the plants will wind around themselves.

4. Plant three begonias at each end of of the planter. The red flowers go well with the red-flowered varieties of pole bean, but you can also team white begonias with white flowers and so on.

5. Protect the plants from slugs, wind, and cold when they are young. Water well.

Dill Pickles to Go

Cucumbers will do well outside in a container, if they are given support and a sunny, sheltered position. Choose an outdoor variety, either one for pickling—this will produce plenty of small fruit to pickle whole—or any other outdoor cucumber. To flavor the pickle, use the growing tips of dill containing the developing flower, stem, and leaves.

You will need

Terra-cotta flowerpot, 12 inches (30 cm) in diameter, 12 inches (30 cm) deep

Drainage material

Potting mix

Supports, such as garden stakes or an obelisk

Bush-type cucumber plant

3 dill plants

Garden twine

Tomato fertilizer

Planting your pot

1. Put some drainage material in the bottom of the pot. Add potting mix, piling it into a slight mound in the center of the pot. Insert a stake or another support. Plant the cucumber in the center of the mound; this will prevent water from rotting the plant and encourage the roots to grow down and seek moisture.

2. Plant young dill plants around the edge of the pot. For a constant supply of young growing tips, sow seeds little and often into small pots as replacements.

3. The young cucumber needs help to attach to the support, so tie on stems using garden twine—eventually, the plant will twine by itself. Cucumber plants are frost sensitive, so harden off plants gradually before planting outside after there is no danger of frost (see page 107).

4. Water the potting mix carefully, at first sparingly because the cucumber stem and roots can rot. Later, once the plant is growing well, water regularly or install an automatic-drip irrigation system. About six weeks after planting, add a tomato fertilizer to promote fruiting. Keep an eye out for powdery mildew; remove and destroy any affected leaves.

5. Cut off the cucumbers at the stem, using a sharp knife or pruners; do not pull them off, or you might dislodge the plant.

How to Grow

Once you have decided where to position the containers and selected some plants to try, it is time to make sure you have all the materials you will need and get started. Growing plants in containers means you don't have to worry about the quality of the soil in the ground (or even the lack of it)—but container growing has its own challenges. Each individual plant has to deliver more in a smaller space—and it needs your help. In this chapter, you'll learn how to get seedlings and plants off to a healthy start and how to keep them that way.

Watering the Plants

All plants in containers will need a regular supply of water, so first choose your water source and decide how you will get it to the plants on a regular basis. This will influence the type, size, number, and position of the containers you will use.

Watering is vital for plants, but watering them can also be a chore. When planning your plantings, think about how you will water your plants. Thinking ahead will make watering your plants easier.

Watering for a few plants

If you plan to grow just a few small to medium plants, one or two watering cans may be all you will need. The right watering can makes all the difference; look for one with a detachable brass "rose," which fits on the end of the spout to break up the stream of water. This gives you three ways to water: with the rose holes pointing upward for gently watering seedlings, the rose holes downward for young plants, and just the spout for quickly watering mature tomatoes or for filling drip trays or reservoirs. Carrying two 1-gallon (4-liter) cans—one in each hand—is easier than one large 2-gallon

The rose on a watering can has holes to break up the water to mimic raindrops.

(8-liter) can, and small watering cans can also be lifted up higher to water wall planters and window boxes.

You may want to consider products available to help reduce the need for watering, such as self-watering containers (see "Choosing Containers," pages 102–103) and adding water-absorbing gels to the potting mix.

Tap water and storing water

An outside faucet, garden hose or two, and some attachments will let you create a watering system tailor-made to your space. For example, a four-way connector will divide the water supply so you can have two water supplies controlled by water timers, leaving separate access to water for manual watering. A wall-mounted reel that rolls up the hose automatically is a great time-saver. If you are using a hose to water plants directly, fit an adjustable spray attachment to control the spray. A watering wand attachment provides extra reach (about 2½–3 feet/75–90 cm) for hanging baskets and window boxes.

Collecting rainwater from the roof of any building, including sheds, via gutters and storing it in a water barrel is a good source of water, as long as the roof does not have asphalt or composite tiles. Raise the barrel up on bricks or another building material so you can easily get a watering can under the faucet at the bottom. The water barrel needs a lid to keep insects and debris out; designs low enough for children to fall into need childproof lids.

Watering via drip feeds

An efficient way of watering is to have a series of hoses with microtubing that emit drips of water attached to each container. These drip irrigation systems are almost always used in conjunction with an automatic timer. You can either buy a kit of hoses, microtubing, and connectors, set up the system, and then position the containers around it according to what the kit can accommodate. Or you can decide what containers you want and where to place them, then measure what you need and order a custom-made system. Whichever method you choose, it is easy to install after a little planning and setup time. It will be worth the effort in the time saved if you were to manually water the plants.

Avoiding extremes

Even if it rains, you still need to check whether you need to water your plants, because the containers might not be directly in the rain or the leaves might direct the water away from the potting mix. Stick your finger down into the potting mix; if it feels damp, there is no need to water. Even automatic-drip irrigation systems need checking, because the holes can get blocked.

 Grow for it!

Vacation watering

- Ask a friend or neighbor to keep an eye on your plants to keep the potting mix moist.
- Invest in vacation watering systems with a reservoir of water connected to a wick or a network of hoses. These keep potting mix moist during a short break, or try bottles of gel that add moisture to the pot.
- Do not be tempted to leave plant pots in deep trays of water for days, because the potting mix will become sodden and the roots will die.

If you find that watering a number of large plantings with a watering can is time-consuming, a garden hose with a spray attachment is a good option.

Plants are also likely to die from being waterlogged. Be wary of planting small plants in large pots and then overwatering. If you use trays under pots, make sure the pots are not sitting in standing water. Pots may not have drainage holes or the holes might be insufficient. In addition to adding drainage holes, add a layer of drainage material (see pages 108–109) to the bottom of the pot.

Choosing Containers

The price, style, and color of a container is a personal choice—these will not have an impact on the plant's growth. However, when it comes to the structural design and size of a container, these factors can affect a plant's performance.

The size of a container is an important consideration. The bigger the container, the more potting mix it can hold. This reduces the frequency of watering and protects the roots from extremes of heat and cold. However, the trade-off is cost and maneuverability. As a guide, use a minimum of a ½-gallon (2-liter) pot at least 6 inches (15 cm) in diameter for smaller leafy greens and herbs. A 2½-gallon (10-liter) pot (about the size of a small bucket) can support a group of three to five different types of plants. Thirsty plants, such as pole beans, cucumbers, and tomatoes, will benefit from a large 4-gallon (15-liter) container.

Containers with a depth of less than 6 inches (15 cm) will subject plant roots to extremes of waterlogging and drying out. If you use them, the plants will need daily attention. New compact plants have reduced the minimum size of pot required, so feel free to experiment; however, the sizes above should yield good results.

Traditional flowerpots

The shape of the classic terra-cotta flowerpot has evolved over the centuries,

Terra-cotta flowerpots come in a variety of shapes, sizes, and styles, glazed and unglazed. Choose ones in a similar style, or mix and match them.

so it now has enough depth for drainage, but is wide enough at the top for plants to thrive. Over time, unglazed terra-cotta will take on a patina that is often considered more attractive than new pots; this is due to its porous nature. Glazed pots have less porous sides, so they are better at holding water, but the glazing can crack in winter. See the "Material checklist," opposite, for other material choices.

It pays to think ahead when it comes to finding planting containers. You can often find bargains after the growing season. For a less expensive option, consider buckets, storage boxes, or crates; these can be recycled options as long as you are sure they have not been used to store harmful chemicials.

Although flowerpots sold for interior use often look pretty, be wary of using them outdoors. They have no drainage holes and heavy rain can saturate small pots of herbs and kill the roots within a few days. It may be possible to make drainage holes, but these pots usually do not wear well outdoors; they can become disfigured, even fall apart, within months.

Window boxes

Rectangular planters near a window are a popular option. Wood is the most versatile material for a window box, and it can be custom made to fit your window, then painted, stained, or varnished to your taste. Use a solid liner if you want to change old displays easily, or choose a porous liner to allow for drainage, thereby limiting rot.

Securing the boxes depends on how the window opens and whether there is a windowsill. There are options for all possibilities,

but it can take time to locate a supplier; an Internet search will be useful. Also be sure you can reach the plants from the window, or they will be difficult to water.

Grow for it!

Material checklist

- **Fiberglass** Lightweight and frost resistant; it can be molded into different faux finishes, including copper and lead, or with motif patterns. Fiberglass pots are expensive but durable.
- **Metal** Inexpensive metal planters often have sharp edges, rust easily, even if painted, and get too hot for the roots. Well-finished, good-quality containers can work well; if you are on a budget, consider buckets or old preserving pans.
- **Plastic** Inexpensive, lightweight, and often with a good finished appearance, plastic pots have many useful features, such as water reservoirs and drip trays, molded in. Thin plastic does not age well because it can fade, buckle, or split.
- **Terra-cotta** Although widely used for growing plants outdoors, most terra-cotta flowerpots are only frost tolerant, not frost resistant, so glazes flake and crack if left outdoors in winter.
- **Terrazzo** Made of fine marble chips mixed with concrete and polished to a smooth finish, these pots keep the roots cool, but they are expensive and heavy.
- **Wood** Make sure the wood is a rot-resistant type suitable for outdoor use, such as redwood or cedar; glued boxes fall apart. Inspect the joints and knots. End-of-season maintenance, such as refinishing, may be required to keep them looking attractive.
- **Wicker and rattan** Rustic and lightweight, both materials are good for tabletop displays and hanging baskets. They often come already lined, but these are not durable.

Self-watering containers

Plastic containers, usually hanging baskets or window boxes, are now available with built-in water reservoirs. These are filled up through an easy-to-reach tube. Water passes from the reservoir below up a wick to the potting mix.

Such containers need watering two to three times less often than a conventional container of a similar size, so they could be handy for plants that need a moist rooting medium, such as lettuce and Asian greens. However, they do not always provide better results for Mediterranean-type herbs, which prefer drier conditions, and there will be a limit to your choice of container.

Planning ahead

Before you purchase the plants, check that you have any liners, brackets, supports, and drainage material, such as gravel or broken clay pieces (you will need enough to line the bottom 2 inches/5 cm of the pot). Plan to complete any jobs, such as painting supports or attaching brackets to walls, before the plant buying and growing season starts.

Growing from Seeds

Sowing your own seeds instead of buying young started plants is an option, even if you are growing plants in containers instead of directly in the ground. By growing plants from seeds, you'll have a greater choice of varieties.

You can raise many annuals from seeds, but in a small area you should concentrate on a few subjects or you will have too many plants. Any leafy salad greens that you want to harvest a little at a time and often is a good choice to grow from seeds. One or two seed packets at the start of the season will be all you need. Root crops, such as carrots and beets, do not do well when transplanted, and one seed or plant provides you with only one or a small cluster of roots, so start these from seeds. Vigorous crops that grow rapidly, such as beans, are difficult for commercial nurseries to grow and transport to the consumer, so these are another good option to grow from seeds.

Selecting varieties

For a greater choice of varieties, select seeds directly from a mail-order or Internet seed supplier early in the year. Some varieties, or cultivars, have certain attributes that make them useful for growing in a small space because of their size or appearance, such as a compact yellow zucchini, a red-leaved beet, or a purple-podded pea. New varieties with increased disease resistance are also often available only as seeds.

Sowing indoors

You can start tender vegetables that need high temperatures to germinate and a long growing season, such as tomato, corn, eggplant, and pepper, earlier indoors before conditions are ideal outdoors. Grow them on a table by a well-lit windowsill in a heated room. Concentrate on hard-to-obtain varieties, such as heirloom tomatoes, that will not be available as plants from most nurseries.

Sowing outdoors

All you need for hardy plants is a place with good light and frost free, but preferably warmer than the minimum germination temperature. A porch is suitable, and so is a cold frame if you have the space. These plants will grow rapidly and you can move them into containers directly outdoors after as few as four weeks; seed-starting trays are ideal. Sow a couple of seeds per cell and if more than one emerges, use scissors to clip all but the strongest seedling later on.

 Grow for it!

Herbs and flowers from seeds

Some herbs used in cooking are a good choice for sowing from seeds; for example, parsley and cilantro are easy to sow and you can harvest them like cut-and-come again salad greens. You can grow chervil and dill, which are not often sold as plants, from seeds. Basil can be difficult, because it dislikes cold and damp conditions. Unless you can provide 75°F (24°C) for two weeks, buy plants in early summer. Sow edible flowers, such as nasturtiums and marigolds, in small pots or directly into their final containers.

Choose a site by a bright windowsill, but not one in direct sunlight, to get seeds started indoors. Direct sunlight can scorch the seedlings.

Once the outdoor temperature is warm enough, you can sow many seeds directly into their final containers. Push large seeds, such as beans and peas, into the potting mix. Sow smaller seeds, such as carrot, in patches, then thin them out. Seed packets usually give instructions for sowing in rows, but you can adapt them to sowing in pots by spacing the seeds equal distances apart. Follow the packet directions for how deep to cover the seeds in potting mix.

Storing seeds

Store seeds in a cool, dry place. A cookie tin kept indoors will keep seeds fresh for the growing season. Group packets according to the sowing month, and move the seeds you want to sow often forward after each sowing to remind you to resow. To save seeds until the next year, reseal the packets and put in an airtight container with a bag of silica gel, then store in the refrigerator.

Germination temperatures

It is tempting to start sowing early, but sowings made too early often fall prey to cold, rot, or pests. Wait until the temperature of the potting mix in the pot is above 40°F (5°C). The calendar month is only a rough guide to the right time to start sowing—the temperature of the potting mix is a more accurate guide. A soil thermometer is inexpensive and easy to use. Simply insert it into the potting mix at the depth the seeds will be sown. Take readings at the same time first thing in morning. The temperatures below are the minimum for sowing. A higher temperature is fine for all plants except lettuce, where germination is poor over 70°F (21°C).

- **40°F (5°C)** Asian greens, fava bean, lettuce, peas, radish
- **45°F (7°C)** Beet, carrot, onion, Swiss chard
- **55°F (13°C)** Beans, cucumber, squash, corn, tomato, zucchini
- **65°F (18°C)** Eggplant, pepper

Buying Young Plants

Whether you want only a couple of vegetable plants, such as one or two peppers or tomatoes, you don't have time to raise plants from seeds, or you want to fill some space quickly, buying young started plants is a handy solution.

Most of the common vegetables and herbs are available in spring as young started plants, or transplants. The varieties available in garden centers tend to be conventional or they may not be named. There is a wider choice by mail order if you order ahead in winter; however, if you are planning a mixed container, this might not be an option because the plants may not arrive at the same time. Sometimes it is simpler to go to the store to buy a container, potting mix, and a selection of available plants and get started.

When to buy

In most garden centers, young vegetable plants are bought in and displayed throughout the spring. Like bedding plants, many tender vegetable plants are put on sale in early spring, yet they cannot be planted outside until late spring. This makes caring for the young plants a lot more work than necessary, because you have to keep them frost free, and you will probably have to transfer them into larger pots at least once to prevent a disturbance to their growth. However, you will gain little if you wait until the correct time before buying, because the plants should be bought as fresh as possible and top-quality plants soon sell out.

Vegetable plants that produce "fruit," such as eggplants, peppers, and tomatoes, are often sold later as mature plants.

Whether buying started plants from plant sales sponsored by a local community group or from a garden center, look for healthy leaves.

These are a good choice if you are unsure about the varieties, because you can judge for yourself their final size and shape.

Herbs are sold in small pots from early spring. Because most are hardy, this is a good time to buy instead of waiting until bigger, more expensive plants are on sale. However, delay buying tender herbs, such as lemon verbena and basil, until after the last expected frost in your area has passed, if you have nowhere to keep them frost free (in the United States, check your local Cooperative Extension Service). Put a floating row cover, folded over to use at double thickness, over plants at night if there is an unexpected frost. Secure the edges to stop it from blowing away. Special covers are available to protect hanging baskets.

Checking the quality

When buying started plants, always buy freshly delivered stock, because plants soon dry out and deteriorate when kept in starter trays for several weeks. Look for stocky or bushy plants with

When moving a plant into a new pot, always support it at the base, near the top of the soil, and set the plant in the new pot at the same level.

 Grow for it!

Hardening off plants

Plants growing indoors need to be introduced to the outside gradually. After the last expected frost in your area has passed, put the plants outside in a sheltered spot for an hour on the first day and bring them back inside, then increase the time over a week. You can plant hardy plants, such as lettuce, peas, and onions, outside immediately unless they were displayed indoors, in which case they need to be hardened off for a week. Keep tender vegetables, such as zucchini, pole beans, and corn, in a bright, frost-free place, and harden off for 10 days before planting outside after the last frost date. If planting outside is delayed by more than two weeks, transfer them into larger pots or apply a general all-purpose fertilizer. You can use a small cold frame, or "plant house," of glass or plastic with a wood or metal frame to avoid having to move the plants around.

healthy green foliage. Avoid straggly or leggy plants that have been deprived of light. Also avoid plants with unnatural, discolored foliage; this is a sign of stress, frost exposure, or lack of nutrients. Inspect young growth for aphids; these will spread to other plants.

Open started plants delivered by mail order on arrival, and transfer them into larger pots as soon as you can to prevent them from becoming pot-bound (when the roots wrap around themselves in the pot), and put them in a bright, frost-free place. Let the supplier know immediately if there is a quality issue instead of waiting in hope that the plants will pull through.

Planting the Containers

By taking a few easy steps to prepare the pots, you will be giving your plants the best start and make them easier to care for later—whether you sow seeds or introduce young started plants to their final containers.

Container planting usually begins in the spring months. Start with the hardy plants, such as perennial herbs, strawberries, beets, lettuce, garlic, and onions, and save the tender ones, such as tomatoes, beans, eggplant, zucchini, and basil, until last. If you have a light, frost-free space, use it to get a head start with crops that need a long growing season, such as corn.

Make sure the containers and potting mix are at a comfortable height. If using small pots, work on a bench or table; if you are using large ones, kneeling down instead of bending over is more comfortable. Put hanging planters in buckets while planting to keep them from tipping over.

Liners and drainage

If a container will rot or discolor when in contact with damp potting mix or if the sides are open, such as a crate or an open mesh basket, you will need to line the container. Use thick plastic, coir matting, or burlap. Use a sharp utility knife to make some drainage slits, but do not trim the edges until a few days after planting because the wet potting mix will pull it down.

Check that the container has enough drainage holes. Use a power drill to make more in the bottom of wooden, plastic, metal, or fiberglass planters. Terra-cotta or glazed pots usually have one centered hole. Cover it with a piece of wire mesh or newspaper so the potting mix won't be washed straight through.

In the days when all pots were made of clay, pieces of broken clay pots were used as a drainage material. You can still use broken pieces of clay pots or china.

 Grow for it!

Potting mixes

The smaller the pot, the better quality the potting mix you need. For large planters, the potting mix quality is less critical. You can use garden soil to supplement more expensive potting mix, but finish with a layer of fresh potting mix to suppress any weed seeds.

- Multipurpose potting mix is convenient and all edibles will do well in it; you can use a fertilizer to provide extra nutrients. All the plantings grown for this book were raised in a peat-free potting mix. If you bought a compressed type, break it up with your fingers and fluff it up. Coir-based mixes may need straining to remove long fibers if you are using it in small pots.
- For long-term plantings, such as roses or strawberries, a soil-based mix lasts longer. Soil mixes are heavy, so for roof gardens or balconies use clay aggregates or perlite mixes.
- Lemon plants need a lime-free citrus mix with matching fertilizer, usually available from an on-line source.

Preparing the container before planting

Start by adding a layer of drainage material. You can break up pieces of terra-cotta pots or china with a hammer; wear gloves and goggles. Alternatively, use small stones or gravel or even packing peanuts or pieces of Styrofoam from bedding trays. You can put the drainage material into mesh bags so it is easy to remove at the end of the season. Drainage material can be kept in containers year after year.

In small pots, the potting mix needs to hold moisture without waterlogging; add preferably organic, moisture-retaining granules to help hold in the moisture without the soil becoming waterlogged. For any size container, fill it halfway with the potting mix.

Sowing seeds and preparing started plants

You can sow seeds into containers of moist potting mix. Most packets have instructions on seed depth and spacing but they assume you will be sowing in rows in the ground. Sow in rows in square planters with 4 inches (10 cm) between rows and harvest younger. In round pots, scatter the seeds over the surface thinly, lightly cover with potting mix, and thin out later as they grow.

Water plants well before transplanting them, and be sure they are hardened off first (see page 107) if the container is going outside immediately. However, you can plant hanging baskets and pouches earlier, when the plants are smaller, and keep them in a bright and frost-free place.

Moving a plant into a larger pot

1 Remove a plant from its original pot by tapping the side of the pot to loosen the soil and then carefully sliding the pot from the roots, making sure the other hand is supporting the plant at its base.

2 Position the plant in the new container at the same level that it was in the original pot. Pack in the potting mix around it and firm in gently, pushing the mix into corners if there are any; if you leave air gaps, the roots will dry out.

3 Once the plant is in, fill in around it and the edge of the pot with more potting mix. Leave a 1-inch (2.5-cm) gap between the surface of the potting mix and the rim; this lets water seep down instead of running off the top.

Caring for Your Crops

Once the container plantings have been assembled, the plants should grow rapidly and be ready for harvesting within weeks. There are just a couple of things to keep in mind to get the best results.

When growing plants in pots, keeping the potting mix consistently moist but not waterlogged is key. This is not as obvious as it sounds; for example, during rainy periods, containers very close to the house can remain dry or, if there are big leaves, the water may run off and never reach the roots. Conversely, heavy rain can saturate a potting mix and starve the roots of air—that is why drainage holes and materials are so important. If you use a saucer under the flowerpot, make sure it doesn't sit full of water for days at a time. When a potting mix is extremely dry, it can be difficult to rewet because the water runs along the side of the pot. In such cases, submerge small pots in clean water with one or two drops of dish soap until they stop bubbling, then let drain. Reduce the need for watering by moving plants into the next pot size up, so there is a greater volume of potting mix, or move pots to a cooler, shadier spot. You will need to arrange some care, or a watering system, for container plants when you go on vacation.

Applying a strip of copper tape around the top edge of a flowerpot can keep slugs and snails away from tempting leaves and other plant morsels.

Fertilizing plants

The nutrients in the potting mix will last for only about four weeks. Compound fertilizers have varying proportions of three main nutrients: nitrogen, phosphorus, and potassium, or N, P, and K. A "balanced" all-purpose fertilizer has an equal amount of these three nutrients and is a good choice for root vegetables, such as beets. It will be labeled as NPK 7-7-7. The numbers reflect the balance of the nutrients, with a high number indicating a higher amount of that particular nutrient, so a fish fertilizer of 2-4-1 has more nitrogen and phosphorus than potassium.

Leafy crops need more nitrogen, so a fertilizer with a higher ratio of nitrogen is best for them. Plants that will benefit from a high-nitrogen fertilizer include Asian greens and spinach. You can also apply it to celery, beans, garlic, kale, lettuce and other salad greens, onions, and shallots if they look in need of help. A tomato fertilizer has little nitrogen and a higher amount of potassium to encourage fruit production. As well as being suitable for tomatoes, a high-potassium fertilizer is good for all "fruiting" vegetables, such as cucumbers, eggplants, peppers, and zucchini.

Because the aim is to eat the plants you are growing, consider using organic fertilizers. These are made from once-living things, such as bonemeal or fish emulsion, or from another natural source, such as rock phosphate. A fertilizer with seaweed extract will also contain trace elements. Whichever type of fertilizer you decide to use, always follow the package directions carefully for applying it; a liquid fertilizer, for example, may need diluting. Carrots, corn, fennel, peas, radishes, and most Mediterranean herbs do better without fertilizer.

Pests

Slugs and snails are a main concern, and attacks are worse during mild, damp conditions. Young leafy crops are the most vulnerable early on and "fruiting" vegetables are attacked in summer and fall. Organic slug pellets are a popular control method because they are inexpensive and easy to apply. Moving containers off the ground, onto tables, for example, can help make it difficult for the slugs and snails to find them.

Grow for it!

Making the most of the space

Unlike purely ornamental container plants, which can flower until the first fall frost, you may need to fill gaps from early summer onward after harvesting edible crops. Have a selection of reserves in small pots ready to go in, and keep them somewhere unobtrusive but where you will remember to water them.

If you have little space, how about a window box on the garden shed or even a garage or a table with shelves outside the back door? After harvesting an early summer (June) crop, such as shallots, early potatoes, or lettuce, follow them with tender vegetables started off in indoor pots, such as zucchini, tomatoes, corn, or bush beans. Later in the summer, during July, plant Asian greens outside to replace those harvested in early summer.

Healthy, tasty edibles, such as these mizuna leaves, will be the result if you care for your plants as they grow.

Aphids can suck the sap from plants, which are then weakened, and the yield can be affected. Some aphids spread viruses from one plant to another; for example, mosaic virus can be introduced into a zucchini plant, which will wither and die. A well-aimed strong jet of water can knock off aphids, but only try this on mature, well-rooted plants. Early in the year, a floating row cover will protect plants from aphids, as well as carrot rust fly and cabbage white butterflies. Later in summer, use a fine plastic netting. Weigh down the edges so pests cannot get in. You can wash and reuse the covers, but check them for holes before reusing them.

Diseases

Soil diseases are rare in container growing, assuming you start with potting mix that is fresh or has been used only once for a different crop. Gray mold (*Botrytis*) can be a problem, so use clean water and moisten the potting mix, not the leaves, flowers, or fruits. Remove any dead or rotting plant remains promptly to prevent the disease from spreading. Blight is spread by raindrops, so it can be a problem in tomatoes and potatoes; bringing them under cover when blight is forecast can help.

What
to Grow

Here's a handpicked selection of vegetables
that will provide the best results in small
spaces. All are annuals, which means they
will grow, produce a crop, and die off in
just one growing season. They need light,
shelter, moisture, and nutrients, plus regular
care from you, to keep them growing
healthily, so check the individual entries
to see what your favorites will need. Salad
greens and leafy vegetables are quick
to grow, but roots, such as carrots, and
"fruiting" plants, such as tomatoes, take
longer—choose a mixture of leafy, root,
and fruiting crops to spread the harvest
over a longer time.

Bush Beans

By far the most hassle-free bean for window boxes, pouches, or hanging baskets, bush beans are neat in habit yet prolific, so you don't even need a yard to grow beans.

Getting started

What to plant Seeds or plants
Site Sunny
When Plant outside in spring after the last frost; sow little and often
Container size 4 plants in a 2½-gallon (10-liter) container
Spacing 5–6 inches (13–15 cm)

Growing bush beans in containers raised off the ground makes them easier to pick than bush beans grown in a garden, and the pods will be a higher quality because they will be lifted away from dirt and slugs. Bush bean varieties with purple and yellow pods will also provide extra ornamental value. However, the green varieties also have their place, because a mixture of yellow and green beans are attractive on the plate. (Purple pods turn to green when cooked.)

Filet beans, which are also called French beans, have long, thin pods that crop extra quickly (48–50 days), and you can start picking them when the pods reach 4 inches (10 cm) long. The purple types, such as 'Royal Burgundy' (60 days) or 'Purple Teepee' (75 days), hold their pods well above their foliage for easier picking.

Round-pod types are plumper and picked when the pods are 6 inches (15 cm) long; 'Blue Lake' (50 days) and 'Tendercrop' (56 days) are typical. For yellow pods, look for a wax bean, such as 'Pencil Pod Wax' (52–60 days). Shelling beans are varieties with larger seeds, such as cranberry beans (70 days), but make sure you get the bush form—not the pole bean of the same name—if you want it for small containers.

Planting

Young started plants are available, but for the greatest choice of ornamental varieties buy seeds from catalogs or an Internet source, and start them in small pots indoors, sowing in batches from March to

Keeping bush beans raised off the ground will mean less backaches when it comes to picking them—and the beans won't pick up dirt.

May. The plants are frost tender but, being small, they fit neatly under a crop cover. To maintain a continuing supply of fresh beans, make additional sowings until early July directly into the growing medium.

Fava beans

Because fava beans are hardier than bush or pole beans and crop early, they are worth considering in areas with a mild winter; however, they are not the neatest or the most productive of beans for containers. Look for bush varieties, such as 'The Sutton' (84 days), which grows to 2 feet (60 cm) and needs only minimum support. The early flowers will also attract beneficial insects.

Seeds normally germinate at 50°F (10°C), producing an early crop around June in an open, sunny site with shelter from strong winds. Simply push four seeds 1½ inches (3.75 cm) deep into a 2½-gallon (10-liter) pot of growing medium in midspring. If it is dry when the flowers form, water well once a week to improve the quality of the final crop. When the plants are in full flower, pinch off the top 4 inches (10 cm) of each plant. This encourages the pods to form and, because this is where aphids gather, it also gets rid of the pests. You can remove the plants after harvesting and replace them with late-flowering perennials, such as penstemons.

Pick the lower pods first as they mature. For shelling, pick the pods when the seeds inside are just showing and are still soft. You can also pick young, tender pods and eat them whole. Note that some people of African, Mediterranean, or Southeast Asian descent have an allergic reaction to raw fava beans and should avoid eating them.

The seeds germinate best at 55°F (13°C); sow one seed per 3-inch (7.5-cm) pot. Sow a few extra pots to allow for any failures. Once their roots have almost filled the pot, harden them off (see page 107) and plant them outside into their final container. To grow as a single planting, allow four plants to a 12-inch (30-cm)-diameter pot.

Care

When the first flowers start to form, keep the growing medium moist to increase the harvest. If you grow them in an exposed site, the plants may need a little support to stop them from flopping over. Use small birch twigs to support them or string tied around stakes pushed into the pot.

Harvesting

Once the pods start to form, pick all the 4–6-inch (10–15-cm)-long pods. If you let the seeds start to mature in unpicked pods, flowering will begin to decline. To prolong the harvest, pick any surplus pods and freeze those you cannot eat. The plants will provide a crop for about three weeks.

To pick a bean, snap each bean off, using your finger and thumb, or snip it off with a pair of scissors. Avoid pulling them off because this will dislodge the plant and damage the roots. Fresh beans are one of the best crops to grow for freezing— simply blanch and freeze (see "Freezing,"

page 117). Leave shelling beans to dry and ripen naturally. Cover the plants during wet spells or bring them indoors to dry in a sunny, airy room. Eventually, the pods will be dry and brittle, and then you can easily separate the seeds and store them in screw-top jars.

When the beans are long enough for harvesting, you may need to pick them as often as every other day when the plants are at their peak.

Pole Beans

Not only are pole beans attractive annual climbers with colorful flowers, they also make excellent use of vertical space and produce large quantities of beans.

Getting started

What to plant Seeds or plants
Site Sunny or partial shade, sheltered from winds
When Plant outside in spring after the last frost
Container size 2 or 3 plants in a 2½-gallon (10-liter) pot
Spacing 6 inches (15 cm) apart

Plant two seeds together to make sure you have a plant. If both seeds happen to germinate, you can let them both grow together.

Pole beans were first grown as ornamentals before it was discovered you could eat the beans. They provide a pretty summer screen, which is useful in an urban or small yard for privacy, but position them where they will not cast shadows over other crops.

For colorful flowers, choose bicolors, such as the red-and-white 'Painted Lady' (85 days), which stand out as eye-catching varieties. For red flowers, consider scarlet runner beans; for purple flowers and pods, try 'Purple Peacock' (70 days). Other pole beans with purple pods include 'Purple King' (75 days) and 'Triumfo Violetta' (75 days), which is an heirloom variety. Yellow pod types include the early 'Marvel of Venice' (54 days) and 'Kentucky Wonder Wax' (70 days). 'Red Noodle' (85 days) has dark burgundy pods. You can also try a yard-long bean, such as 'Gita' (78 days), which produces 16–20-inch (40–50-cm)-long, stringless green pods.

Dwarf varieties are handy for containers where a tall support is not feasible. They are still taller than bush beans, so they will need some support from stakes (twigs are also handy); 'Hestia' (70 days) has attractive red-and-white bicolor flowers.

Planting

You will need a large planter or half barrel with garden stakes or a long, rectangular planter with a trellis panel or a similar built-in support. An alternative is to grow the beans in a long, rectangular planter against a sunny wall covered with netting. The stakes need to be 6–8 feet (1.8–2.4m) tall in a 2–3-foot (60–90-cm)-diameter container. Tie the top ends together—use garden

Shelling and drying

Shelling beans are a halfway house between fresh and dry beans. They are left in the pod to swell, then shelled and used before they dry. Grow beans for drying in the warmest spot so they can dry as much as possible on the plant. If rain is in the forecast, either cut the dried stems and bring them inside, or untie the beans, lay them down on a sheet of plastic, and put a rainproof floating cover over them. When they are completely dried, remove the pods and shake out the dried beans. Remove any damaged ones and store the rest in airtight jars. You can store the beans along with clean pods, or shell them and store in a vermin-proof container. Soak overnight before cooking.

Freezing

At their peak of cropping, even a few bush bean or pole bean plants can produce more beans than you can eat fresh. The best way to preserve fresh beans is to freeze them. Choose the best-quality beans and aim to freeze the beans the same day you pick them. Bring a large saucepan of water to a boil and prepare a bowl of cold, iced water. Pick the beans, clean, trim off the ends, and slice, if they are large. Place them in a steamer basket, plunge it into boiling water for 2–3 minutes, then plunge it into the iced water for 2–3 minutes and drain. Divide the beans into meal-size servings and put into freezer bags or containers. Label and date them; use within four to six months.

string or wire, or make an attractive feature by being creative with the material and method you use to secure the stakes. To grow pole beans up a fence, trellis, arch, or pergola, use netting to help support them.

Sow two seeds to a 5-inch (13-cm) pot. Keep the pots at 50–54°F (10–12°C). If both germinate, do not separate them but plant both together. Continue to grow them at a minimum temperature of 45°F (7°C) until they are 6–8 inches (15–20 cm) tall.

Gradually harden off young plants (see page 107) to prepare them for planting outside. You can also sow the seeds directly into containers after the danger of late frost has passed. Sow ¾ inch (2 cm) deep when the growing medium is 50°F (10°C).

Sow or plant two or three plants to a 2½-gallon (10-liter) pot. Sow or plant two seeds to each support at 6-inch (15-cm) intervals.

Care

In exposed areas, protect young plants from cold winds until they are well established. If the first shoots flop, wind them counterclockwise around the support and tie them in. Eventually, the plants will cling onto the supports by themselves.

Water the growing medium regularly in dry weather. Give generous soakings to encourage flowering and increase the size of the pods. When the plants reach the top of their supports, pinch off their growing tips; this will encourage the formation of side shoots.

Protect plants from slugs by wrapping copper tape around the pot. Aphids can build up rapidly in the summer, stunting the plants and reducing the crop. Natural enemies, such as ladybugs, will help keep them under control. If not, you can spray with an insecticide soap; follow the package directions carefully.

Flowers sometimes fail to produce pods. Cool spells may discourage pollinating insects, or high nighttime temperatures or drought can cause the embryo beans to abort. Water the soil in hot, dry weather, but do not spray the flowers.

When pole beans are ready to harvest, pick every bean, even if you cannot eat or freeze them all, to prolong cropping into late summer.

Harvesting

Pick the beans when they are 3–6 inches (7.5–15 cm) long. If they grow too large, they will become tough and stringy, and there will be a decrease in the crop. To check, the bean should snap cleanly without any string. Before you go on vacation, pick even the tiniest beans and flowers so you have a continuing crop when you return.

Beets

These sweet-tasting roots really earn their keep in a small space. Both the leaves and roots can be eaten, and you can leave them planted in the container until needed.

The flavor of baby beets is at its best when the roots are the size of a golf ball.

Getting started

What to plant Seeds
Site Sunny or partial shade; rich growing medium
When Sow in early spring, in small amounts every two weeks for baby beets, until midsummer
Container size Any for baby beets
Spacing Sow seeds 1–2 inches (2.5–5 cm) apart

For baby beets, look for quick-maturing varieties, such as 'Red Ace' (50 days) or 'Detroit Dark Red' (60 days). 'Bull's Blood' (70 days) has bright red foliage; you can use its young leaves in salads (the roots are disappointing). For beets served as a vegetable, try the golden yellow roots of 'Burpees Golden' (55 days), or try 'Chioggia' (54 days)—its rings of red and white will blend to pink when cooked.

Planting

For quick, even germination, soak seed "clusters" (beet seeds are not true seeds but a dried fruit with several seeds) in warm water overnight before sowing. Sow two seed clusters in a 3-inch (7.5-cm) pot 1 inch (2.5 cm) deep. Keep the pots somewhere cool but frost free. Beets will germinate at 50°F (10°C). When the clump of seedlings have their first true leaves, transfer them as a clump to their final container and space the clumps 6 inches (15 cm) apart.

Or, if growing as a single planting, sow directly in the final container, placing a seed cluster 2 inches (5 cm) apart each way.

For a supply of baby beets, sow at regular intervals in spring and summer. If you are growing beets for storage, sow once in summer (May–June) and harvest from August or September onward. Pull every other root as a baby beet, and let the remainder grow to full size for winter storage.

Care

Keep the growing medium evenly moist. Watering, or even heavy rain after a dry spell, will cause the roots to split. Feed with a balanced all-purpose fertilizer biweekly. Even if insects attack the leaves, the roots will still be edible. Pick off and destroy severely affected leaves.

Harvesting

After the plants have been growing for four weeks, you can pick a few young leaves from each plant to use in salads. Later on, older leaves are a good spinach substitute. Harvest the first baby beets when 1 inch (2.5 cm) in diameter. Twist off the leaves but keep the thin taproot intact. (This helps prevent the color from bleeding during cooking.) You can keep beets in the ground until the first frost, when the ground freezes. Pull the beets when 2 inches (5 cm) in diameter. Rinse the beets in water to clean them before cooking them in their skins, then rub the skins off. Store beets in a refrigerator for up to three weeks in a plastic bag. The leaves will stay fresh for a week.

Bok Choy & Asian Greens

In the right conditions, bok choy and other Asian greens are attractive and quick crops that provide salad greens, cooked greens, and stir-fry ingredients, all from the same container.

Getting started

What to plant Seeds
Site Cool partial shade; rich, moist growing medium
When Early spring or late summer
Container size Any
Spacing 1 inch (2.5 cm) apart and thin to 8 inches (20 cm)

In the category of Asian greens, seed companies list many types of fast-growing edible leaves, often combined in a mix with bok choy, recognizable by its head of white stems with bright green, broad leaves. Mizuna has deeply serrated leaves, while

The fleshy white stems of mature bok choy add crunch to a salad. The leaves are ideal in stir-fries.

mibuna has more rounded leaves. When young, they have a mild mustard flavor, which develops into a stronger, rougher flavor. Both mature in only 40 days. Mustards are even hotter in flavor and the red-purple varieties are attractive plants.

Planting

Asian greens are a good crop to plant after lettuce, spinach, or arugula, because you can sow them in late summer for a fall crop. Bok choy grows best in cool conditions in a moist growing medium. In cool areas, sow in early spring and repeat in July for a fall crop. In mild or warm regions, sow in late summer. In cold areas, sow the seeds in divided seed-starting trays four weeks before the last frost, then harden off (see page 107) before moving outside. Sow a seed ½ inch (1 cm) deep every 1 inch (2.5 cm) and thin out in stages by removing every other plant for baby leaves and letting others grow bigger. For only mature plants, sow seeds 8 inches (20 cm) apart or according to the packet directions; varieties do vary.

The pointy leaves of the fast-growing mizuna are either green, as above, or a red-purple color.

Care

These plants grow rapidly, so most of the care is aimed at keeping the growing medium moist to prevent the plant from producing flowers (bolting) instead of leaves. Feed with a balanced all-purpose fertilizer every two weeks. Many pests, such as flea beetle, are attracted to these plants, so protect them with a floating row cover.

Harvesting

Pick young leaves for salad greens or let the plants reach full size. Cut the plant to 1 inch (2.5 cm) above soil level and let the stump regrow a second flush of leaves.

Carrots

Sweet and crunchy baby carrots are ideal for containers, and their feathery foliage is an attractive feature that works well with patio flowers.

Regular, full-size carrots need a deep planter and are slower growing, but they are a better choice if you want to store carrots for the winter.

Getting started

What to plant Seeds or seed tape
Site Sun; sandy growing medium
When April, then every 6–8 weeks until August
Container size At least 12 inches (30 cm) deep
Spacing Sow seeds 1 inch (2.5 cm) apart; thin to 1 inch (2.5 cm)

Early varieties (ready in 50 days) produce a usable root quickly, so they are the best types to sow in spring for the earliest crop of carrots. You can also sow them regularly throughout the season for a succession of baby carrots or leave them to mature for winter use. Any 'Amsterdam' type will quickly produce thin roots in 55 days that children love to eat raw. 'Nantes' carrots (65–70 days), with 6-inch (15-cm)-long roots, are easy to prepare for cooking. 'Chantenay' types (70 days) form short, broad roots. Round types, such as 'Parmex' (50 days), are good for shallow containers.

Planting

Scatter the seeds thinly—aim for a seed every 1 inch (2.5 cm)—on moist growing medium. Cover with a ¼–½-inch (5–10-mm) layer of growing medium. Use seed tape, where the seeds are sandwiched between long paper strips, if handling the tiny seeds is awkward. The seeds are slow to germinate, but they will grow once the temperature reaches 41°F (5°C). When the seedlings are big enough to handle, gently pull out extra seedlings so plants are 1 inch (2.5 cm) apart.

Care

Carrots growing in containers need regular watering in dry spells to keep the soil moist. Sow an early variety every six to eight weeks for a continuing supply of baby carrots. Pull early sowings before they get too big.

Carrot rust fly grubs can tunnel into the roots and ruin the crop. The adult flies usually fly close to the ground in their quest for carrots, so lifting a container 2½ feet (75 cm) off the ground or using a floating row cover will help keep the flies from reaching the plants. Because the flies are attracted to the smell of pulled carrots, thin and harvest carrots in the evening, when the flies are not active.

Harvesting

If the roots do not slide out when you pull the bottom of the leaves gently, use a hand fork to ease them out. To store for a few days, cut off the leaves or the roots will shrivel.

Storing carrots in winter

In early summer, make one sowing of a full-size carrot variety, such as 'Danvers' (75 days) or 'Purple Haze' (70 days). Thin out the carrots to 2–3 inches (5–7.5 cm) between plants. In the fall, lift the roots. To store carrots, layer them in single rows between slightly moist sand in wooden boxes and keep them in a cool, dark place.

Cucumbers

Imagine picking a fresh cucumber every day throughout the summer from one or two plants growing in containers near your kitchen door.

Getting started

What to plant Seed or plants
Site Warm, full sun, in well-drained growing medium
When Plant outside in late spring after the last frost
Container size 2½-gallon (10-liter) container for modern bush types; at least 4-gallon (15-liter) container for vine types
Spacing 12–18 inches (30–45 cm) apart

The modern bush varieties have a compact habit ideal for containers, but you can grow even rampant vine types in a large pot or rectangular planter with a trellis for support.

There are many new varieties; 'Bush Champion' (55 days) is a compact bush plant that produces plenty of cucumbers. Good pickling varieties include 'Alibi' (55 days) with 4-inch (10-cm)-long cucumbers and 'Burpee Pickler' (53 days).

Planting

In warm areas, insert the seeds into the growing medium once the soil temperature is 65°F (18°C). In cool areas with a short growing season, start off seeds in individual pots indoors at a temperature of 70°F (21°C). After there is no more danger of frost, harden off the plants gradually before moving them outside into their final pots. Pile the growing medium into a slight mound in a pot before planting a cucumber; this prevents the plant from rotting in water.

Care

After first planted outside, keep watering to a minimum. Make sure the pots have

Water cucumber plants only in the morning to avoid wet soil overnight because plants are prone to rot.

Once the cucumbers form, make sure you regularly pick them, at least twice a week, to help keep the plants producing more cucumbers.

adequate drainage. Once the plants are established, water regularly or install an automatic-drip irrigation system. About six weeks after planting, feed with a tomato fertilizer to promote the development of cucumbers. Keep an eye out for powdery mildew, and remove and destroy any affected leaves.

Harvesting

Pick slicing cucumbers when 6–8 inches (15–20 cm) long, usually every other day. Pickling varieties are ready when 3–4 inches (7.5–10 cm) long.

Eggplant

With their large, soft leaves, purple flowers, and eye-catching crop, eggplants are ornamental container plants suitable for any sunny patio or deck.

As long as you position the plant in a warm, sheltered spot, you will have a wonderful display of eggplants as attractive as any flowers.

Getting started

What to plant Seeds or plants
Site Warm, full sun and shelter
When Plant outside in late spring after the last frost
Container size At least 12 inches (30 cm) in diameter
Spacing 1 plant per pot

Top-heavy eggplants need a heavy ceramic or terra-cotta pot. They are best as a single planting because they need all the sun possible, and they need staking. However, you can add a quick crop of arugula or herbs before the eggplants start to flower.

Eggplants come in many sizes, shapes, and colors. The small or egg-shape ones are the easiest to manage in flowerpots because the weight of long eggplants can cause the container to overturn and be easily damaged. Pretty varieties include: 'Fairy Tale' (65 days), with 4-inch (10-cm), white-and-purple striped eggplants and stems that are less spiny than some; 'Kermit' (60 days) has small, round green-and-white mottled eggplants 2 inches (5 cm) wide. In warm areas, 'Rosa Bianca' (75 days) produces white-and-mauve striped eggplants. In northern areas where the growing season is shorter, try 'Dusky' (63 days), with dark purple eggplants.

Collecting eggplant seeds

Because eggplant varieties don't often cross-pollinate, it's possible to collect seeds by letting one or two of the eggplants grow until completely mature, past it's edible stage. Remove the seeds, let dry, and store in a dark, cool place in an airtight container for up to four years.

Planting

Seeds need to be started early in the year in warm conditions, so it is easiest to buy young plants in late spring. However, you can sow seeds in small pots and maintain them at 80°F (27°C). Gradually harden off (see page 107) young plants, waiting until well after the last frost before planting outside—the growing medium needs to be 70°F (21°C) before planting into it.

Care

Once the plants are well-established, water and feed with a tomato fertilizer to keep the plant producing eggplants. It is usually necessary to stake the plants. Spider mites can turn leaves yellow, but misting or spraying foliage with a strong jet of water can dislodge them.

Harvesting

Cut off the first eggplant when it reaches half of its full size. The flesh will be sweet and tender and, by removing one early, you will encourage more eggplants to form. Some varieties have spines on their stems, so harvest carefully.

Kale

A hardy leafy vegetable with an attractive texture and high in nutrients, young kale leaves can be eaten as a salad green, and later on, mature leaves make tasty steamed greens.

If you live in a cold area, plant kale in a raised bed or large frost-resistant container.

Getting started

What to plant Seeds or plants
Site Cool partial shade in a growing medium rich in organic matter
When Early spring and midsummer to early fall
Container size Any for salad greens; 3 feet (90 cm) in diameter for winter vegetable
Spacing Plant 6–18 inches (30–45 cm) apart

Once a humble winter green, kale has now been rediscovered as an ornamental edible leaf. There are varieties with red leaves, such as 'Redbor' and 'Red Russian' (both 55 days), and green, such as 'Winterbor' (60 days), as well as Italian heirloom types, such as 'Black Kale' (125 days) with blue-green straplike foliage.

Kale thrives in cool areas and is hardy. When growing in containers, however, be sure the roots do not freeze.

Planting

For a few plants to fill a container, start the seeds off in 3-inch (7.5-cm) flowerpots. The seeds are large and easy to handle. Sow two seeds per flowerpot (or peat pots to prevent root disturbance). If both seeds germinate, remove the weaker one. (If they are close together, snip it off with scissors.)

Grow the young plants in the pots in a sheltered spot outdoors in a cool but frost-free place. Use a fine mesh floating row cover to protect them from pests, such as flea beetle. Slugs may also damage the young plants. If the leaves start to change color, the plants may be running out of nutrients. Give them a balanced all-purpose fertilizer, or transplant them into a larger pot. (Don't remove the plants from peat pots; just plant the peat pots into the larger pots.)

Transplant into a larger container or raised bed in midsummer. First water the pot or raised bed well. Make a slight depression and plant into the bottom. This allows for easier watering in a dry summer, until the plants are established.

For container growing, use a flowerpot that holds at least 1½ gallons (6 liters) of growing medium and position it where you can water it frequently. You can grow smaller varieties as baby vegetables planted as close as 6 inches (15 cm) apart; set other plants for mature kale at 18 inches (45 cm) apart.

Care

Make sure the growing medium does not dry out. You can apply fertilizer monthly to encourage rapid growth of young leaves.

Harvesting

Cut leaves as required, but the flavor is better after a frost. Wash thoroughly or soak leaves in salted water for 20 minutes, then rinse to remove insects trapped in the curly leaves. You can let kale overwinter in warm areas if mulched; it may produce flower stalks and tender young leaves in spring.

Lettuce

The amount of lettuce you can grow in even small spaces is astonishing and, with some careful timing of the sowings, you can have your own salad bar on tap all summer.

Getting Started

What to plant Seeds, plants
Site Sun or partial shade; partial shade best in summer
When Sow in early spring, then make frequent small sowings every two weeks
Container size 6–8 inches (15–20 cm) in diameter for a single lettuce; at least 8–9 inches (20–23 cm) in diameter for a mixture
Spacing 5–15 inches (12.5–38 cm) apart, depending on variety

Loose-leaf and compact heads of lettuce are perfect for growing in flowerpots, window boxes, and other containers. They need little care, other than regular watering. By growing your own lettuce from seeds, you will have a greater choice of varieties than what is available at grocery stores. As well as green, you can grow red or bronze-leaved lettuce and many are speckled or streaked with color. The variations of texture and leaf shape add to their appeal, with frills, crinkles, pointed leaves, and oak leaves all adding interest to mixed plantings—and you will have a regular harvest of leaves ready for picking.

Firm heads and loose leaves

Lettuce varieties change frequently, so start by choosing the type you want to grow, such as a lettuce that forms a firm head or frilly loose leaves. Next look at the varieties available within that category, either in seed catalogs or as young started

Young lettuce plants will need room to grow to a larger size, so don't crowd them too closely together.

plants. There are several main categories to choose from.

- Loose-leaf lettuce types produce a lot of leaves but little head. You can cut the outside leaves as needed and leave the rest of the plant to continue growing and supplying new leaves. There are many easy-to-grow varieties. 'Lollo Rossa' has red-tinted edges, and 'Salad Bowl' is a reliable variety; 'Oakleaf' has deeply lobed leaves.

- Butterhead types have round, loose heads and soft-textured leaves with a buttery flavor. 'Tom Thumb' (60 days) is the smallest. 'Cassandra' (70–85 days) is a modern variety with good resistance to fungal disease, while 'Buttercrunch' (65 days) is an older reliable variety.

- Crispheads, or icebergs, are large plants with crinkled outer leaves and a firm, crisp head. 'Mini Green' is a mini crisphead; 'Blush' is similar but has a pink flush.

- Romaine lettuce has long, pointed leaves with a pale, firm head. They are sweet, crunchy, and slow to run to seed. 'Little Gem' (54 days) is a small lettuce suitable for close spacing.

  To grow smaller varieties, space them 5–6 inches (12.5–15 cm) apart. These are a good choice for growing in pots, window boxes, or raised beds. Each plant will make a head about 3 inches (7.5 cm) across, which is ideal for a salad for two.

Planting

Sow seeds directly into the final container, start them in small pots, or buy young started plants. Sow two or three seeds together, about ½ inch (1 cm) deep, in small pots or into a seed starting tray. Let the seedlings grow until they have four leaves, then transplant them into their final containers. Spacing varies from 9 inches (23 cm) to 15 inches (38 cm), depending on the variety, but loose-leaf types can be 5 inches (12.5 cm) apart. Lettuce seeds germinate well at low temperatures, but at 70°F (21°C) or higher, germination is erratic. In warm regions, sow only in spring and fall. In cool areas, keep sowing additional batches at two-week intervals to maintain a constant supply throughout the summer.

Care

A growing medium rich in organic matter will help retain moisture, and a balanced all-purpose fertilizer will help produce a supply of leaves. Lettuce in containers escapes many of the soil pests, but slugs and snails can still be a nuisance. Go out with a flashlight at nighttime to collect and dispose of them. Aphids will attack plants in containers as well as in the vegetable plot, so check the undersides of the leaves occasionally for tiny flies and pick off any affected leaves.

Frilly leaved 'Lollo Rossa' lettuce tinged with bronze makes an attractive feature that can take center stage in a mixed planting.

Harvest lettuce leaves in the early morning, when the leaves are fresh and filled with moisture. As the day continues, they lose moisture and will be limp.

Harvesting

Each sowing of lettuce can provide baby leaves, more mature single leaves, and whole heads of lettuce. You can cut loose leaves from the outer edges with a pair of scissors as needed and use them right away. Whole heads of butterheads and crispheads will keep for a week in a refrigerator. To check that a head of lettuce is ready, lay the back of your hand on top and press gently— it should feel firm. Use a sharp knife to cut at the bottom of the plant.

Mesclun & Salad Green Mixes

Grow a tasty mixture of leafy greens and herbs, so that you can pick the young leaves for a regular supply of fresh salad greens.

Getting started

What to plant Seeds
Site Sun or partial shade
When Spring; then small sowings every two weeks until August
Container size 12 inches (30 cm) in diameter
Spacing Sow seeds ½–1 inch (1–2.5 cm) apart

You can grow almost any edible leaf in a container and harvest it when young, using the increasingly popular "cut-and-come-again" technique. This involves cutting the leaves to about 1 inch (2.5 cm) above soil level, then leaving the stumps for the plants to regrow. The method is ideal for getting a lot of salad greens out of a window box, patio container, or small raised bed.

A good place to start is to try seed mixture packets of edible leaves, often labeled as 'Saladini' or 'Mesclun', which

Growing salad green varieties in different pots makes it easier for you to control the mixture of leaves that ends up on your plate.

usually include lettuce, endive, and chicory plus other species. Or choose your favorite leafy greens and make up a combination yourself, either as a mixture or on its own.

Homemade mesclun mixtures

To create your own mixture, start with a lettuce, such as 'Little Gem', 'Green Salad Bowl', or 'Frisby' to add bulk to a salad. Then add your favorite plants, which may include some of the following:

- Arugula has a distinct peppery, nutty flavor and attractively cut leaves; the plants go to seed quickly, especially in hot weather. Make small sowings every few weeks and pick frequently.

- Spinach lends a mild, buttery taste to the mixture; grow it in spring or fall, because plants tend to bolt in midsummer.

- Mâche (also referred to as corn salad or lamb's lettuce) is slow growing, so it can be swamped by other species; however, it is a hardy type. Mâche has a mild, juicy, and crunchy flavor.

- Asian greens (see page 119), such as bok choy and mizuna, have a mild peppery flavor when young. The Asian mustards have a hotter flavor.

- Chicory and frisée endive add bitter notes—just grow a small amount and pick young.

- To add color, try kale, which has a subtle cabbage flavor (see page 123). You can

Watercress

You might think you need a stream to grow watercress, but you can grow it easily in a container. Place it in partial shade and where you can water it easily. Sow the seeds thinly and cover with ½ inch (1 cm) of growing medium. Water regularly to keep the growing medium moist. Pick the leaves often to stop the plants from running to seed. Growth may slow down during hot periods but will often restart later. Alternatively, try American or upland cress, which will tolerate a drier growing medium and cold weather. Pick the leaves young before the plants start to flower.

also add young beet leaves (see page 118) or red Swiss chard (see page 137).

■ You can grow many herbs that you grow from seeds as cut-and-come-again crops, such as cilantro, basil, and parsley.

Planting

Sow small 4–6-inch (10–15-cm) patches of individual ingredients. Or if you opt for a mixture, sow thinly in bands 4 inches (10 cm) wide or scatter in patches. Leave ½–1 inch (1–2.5 cm) between seedlings.

To grow mesclun in a flowerpot, choose one with a diameter of at least 12 inches (30 cm). Scatter the seeds thinly and cover with ½ inch (1 cm) of growing medium.

To get a head start in spring, the first batch of mesclun in containers can be started off under a floating row cover. Start the seeds in small pots or seed-starter trays on a windowsill for planting outside when conditions are more favorable. Outside, sow in containers and cover them with a floating row cover. You will need a site in full sun for early sowings, but move the containers to a semishaded site in midsummer to produce a better quality harvest.

Sow small amounts at two-week intervals, or wait until one sowing has germinated or reached a certain stage before sowing the next batch. This should help spread them out over the season.

Care

Water the growing medium regularly to keep the seedlings strong; too little water can slow down their growth. Watch out for slugs, snails, and aphids. Apply a balanced all-purpose fertilizer to make sure leaves continue to grow after cutting.

Harvesting

Cut small quantities of leaves, either as whole young plants or as individual leaves, over a couple of weeks. Aim to have another batch coming into production as soon as the previous one is exhausted.

At first, use scissors to cut immature plants or individual leaves as required. Choose the larger leaves from the outside of the plants, leaving small and young

Plant a mixture of salad greens with different leaf shapes, sizes, and textures to create an attractive planting, but make sure the plants don't overcrowd their neighbors.

leaves in the center to continue growing. Later on, when the leaves are about 4 inches (10 cm) long, cut the whole plants, leaving a 1-inch (2.5-cm) stump to regrow in the cut-and-come-again fashion. You should get at least two harvests, and possibly up to four, from a sowing. For really fresh salad greens, pick the leaves at the last minute, wash thoroughly, and spin dry.

Peas

Fresh, sweet peas—whether you eat them whole, pod and all, or shell them—are a real summer treat that is possible whatever growing space you have.

Getting started

What to plant Seeds, started plants
Site Sunny
When Sow in spring where winters are mild, then again in late summer
Container size 12 inches (30 cm) in diameter, to hold 16–24 seeds
Spacing Sow seeds 1 inch (2.5 cm) apart

You can grow tall climbing peas in pots with tepees or in large, rectangular planters with a trellis or netting attached to a nearby fence or wall. Or plant a bush variety into a

In cold areas, start seeds indoors in 3-inch (7.5-cm) pots before moving them outdoors to larger pots.

pot or hanging basket. Tall varieties usually have a longer harvesting period than the shorter varieties from a single sowing. Make several sowings of a short variety every 10 days or make a sowing of an early variety as well a regular season variety.

Peas and pods

There are different types of peas to choose from. The thick fleshy pods of snap peas, also called sugar peas, are sweet and crunchy. 'Sugar Snap' (68 days) grows to 6 feet (1.8 m) but there are varieties under 3 feet (1 m), such as 'Sugar Ann' (55 days).

Snow peas have flat pods and should be picked before the peas develop. You can eat them raw in salads or cook them briefly in stir-fries. 'Oregon Sugar Pod' (68 days) is a typical 30-inch (75-cm)-high variety, but there are tall heirloom ones, too.

Shelling garden peas are grown for the peas, not the pods, which have thin walls. Most are vine types. An increasingly popular trend is to eat the tendrils and pea shoots of the plants. There are now varieties, such

Make a tepee in a large planter, using tall poles or stakes held by twine, for vining peas to climb up.

as 'Feisty' (10 days for shoots, 61 days for peas), with more tendrils than leaves.

Planting

Peas don't like heat, so sow seeds early (at 40–50°F/4–10°C). In hot areas, sow in early spring. You can try sowing in late summer.

Grow eight plants to a 2½-gallon (10-liter) container, sowing a few more seeds to allow for failures. All but the smallest varieties will need support of either branched brush—use 2-foot (60-cm)-long winter prunings from live hardwood shrubs—or netting securely tied to posts. Put the supports in place in the containers before or shortly after the seedlings emerge. Plant tall varieties 5 inches (12.5 cm) apart near their supports.

Care

The plants should cling to the supports, but you may need to tie them in. If the soil is dry, watering well when the plants are in full flower and the first pods starting to form will increase the yield.

Harvesting

The earliest crop should be ready in late spring to summer. Snow peas should have flat pods 2 inches (5 cm) long with immature peas inside. Both the peas and pods should be thick in snap peas. If either type is left too long, they will be stringy and tough. Shelling peas should have uncrowded, round peas. Go over the plants every day or two, picking all pods that are ready. Leaving pods on the plants for too long will shorten the cropping season.

Peas are truly attractive plants whose delicate tendrils, delightful flowers, and attractive foliage all add to their charm.

Peppers

You can easily train both sweet peppers and chilies into neat, bushy plants that will produce enough ripe peppers to more than pay for a prime site on the patio.

Getting started

What to plant Started plants
Site Sunny and warm; sheltered
When Plant outside after the last frost
Container size Minimum of 8 inches (20 cm) in diameter, but depends on variety
Spacing At least 8 inches (20 cm) apart, but depends on variety

Chili plants are particularly decorative and just one plant should keep even an enthusiastic chili lover supplied all winter. Sweet peppers are larger plants but they produce fewer peppers, so you will need three plants to supply an average family. It is easiest to start with young plants because the seeds need starting early in the year at high temperatures. Plants are frost sensitive, so they need hardening off (see page 107) before moving them outside.

Whether you prefer hot or sweet peppers, they come in an amazing array of varieties: from left to right are an ornamental chili 'Medus' with upright chilies, a cayenne chili with chilies that are ideal for drying, a yellow sweet bell pepper, the sweet pepper 'Sweet Banana', and chili 'Hungarian Hot Wax'. Whatever type of peppers you grow, harvest them in the same way—use a sharp knife or pruners to cut a chili or sweet pepper from the plant.

Pepper types

Most peppers and chilies do well in pots, but look for compact varieties. If growing sweet bell peppers, consider 'Redskin', an early-cropping type, or 'Purple Star', which produces deep purple peppers.

Besides the typical blocky bell pepper shape, there are other types of sweet peppers, classified by their shape. Some have long, slender, pointy shapes; others are a more cylindrical shape. 'Corno di Toro' refers to the "bull's horn" shape of the pepper. Cherry peppers have small peppers.

Chilies also come in different shapes, but the amount of heat is a more important consideration. Habanero peppers tend to be especially hot, while 'Zavory' is a mild variety. 'Anaheim' produces long, mild-to-medium hot chilies. 'Cayenne' is a compact type with very hot, twisted, thin peppers.

Planting

As the plants begin to fill their small pots, transfer them into ½-gallon (2-liter) pots. When these begin to fill, move the plants into 1½-gallon (6-liter) pots. When the plants reach 8 inches (20 cm) high, pinch off the growing tip with your finger and thumb to encourage the plants to form a bushy habit.

Care

Sweet peppers may need support once the peppers start to swell, but chilies should remain bushy. As the plants flower and the vegetables mature, you may need to water the plants twice a day on hot days; a lack of moisture when the flowers are forming will cause black rot on the peppers. Feed when the first flowers start to form and again in three weeks with a tomato fertilizer.

Harvesting

Peppers and chilies can be cut off the plants at any stage. Green peppers are less sweet and green chilies less hot than when completely ripe; however, cutting them early will encourage the plant to produce more. Peppers and chilies will keep for up to 10 days in the refrigerator.

Drying and freezing

You will probably use up any sweet peppers you harvest, but even a single chili plant will produce a surplus. In hot areas, you can string up chilies and dry them in the sun before storing; chilies with thin skins dry the best. You can also dry chilies in an oven on its lowest setting for 24 hours or more. Freezing in plastic bags is another alternative.

Potatoes

There's nothing like the taste of your own new potatoes. Growing them in containers is a quick-and-easy way to start that doesn't require digging or soil preparation.

Potato plants produce a canopy of green foliage and some small flowers, but are otherwise unobtrusive; to make a visual impact, choose the planter carefully.

Getting started

What to plant Certified seed potatoes
Site Sunny or partial shade
When Plant in spring; keep frost free
Container size Minimum 2-gallon (8-liter) pot
Spacing 1 tuber per 2-gallon (8-liter) pot

You can grow any potato variety in a planter, but an early season variety will crop quicker and have a neater appearance. Get certified seed potatoes from a garden supplier; supermarket potatoes may carry diseases or be treated with chemicals to stop them from sprouting. As soon as they are purchased, put seed potatoes in a bright, frost-free place, such as on a windowsill, to produce sprouts.

The containers need to be moved at least once from their initial frost-free place to their final growing position outside. Containers with handles that can be dragged into place are handy. A 2½–4-gallon (10–15-liter) container will hold enough potting mix for two to three tubers and three containers of this size will be sufficient. Terra-cotta pots are attractive but budget alternatives

include recycled plastic pots used to sell trees or large planters or large buckets. Potato planter bags are another option.

Planting

Three weeks before the last frost date for your area (March–April), fill your container halfway with a rich potting mix and bury sprouted tubers into the mix. As the tops grow, keep covering them with layers of potting mix until you reach the top of the containers. Potato foliage is frost sensitive, so wait until there is no danger of frost before moving the containers outside.

Care

If a late frost is likely, cover the potatoes with a double layer of floating row cover overnight or move them under cover. Keep the potting mix moist; if too dry, the tubers will not form, but if too wet, they will rot. Keep adding soil mix, but leave a 1-inch (2.5-cm) gap at the top of the planter for watering. Avoid splashing the foliage. During hot or dry spells, move the

containers into partial shade. Fertilizing is not necessary. Do not grow potatoes next to tomatoes; both are prone to blight.

Harvesting

The tubers are ready to harvest when they are the size of a hen's egg; push your hand gently down and feel for the tubers. If you use potato bags, you can feel them through the bag. The easiest way to harvest potatoes is to tip the contents out into a wheelbarrow.

Sweet Potatoes

Nutritious sweet potatoes are versatile tubers from vigorous vines. In warm areas (or if you can provide cover), it is possible to grow them in containers.

Getting started

What to plant Pot-grown plants or certified "slips" (cuttings)
Site Sunny, sheltered from cold winds
When Plant outside in late spring when there is no danger of frost
Container size One plant per 8-gallon (30-liter) pot
Spacing 18 inches (45 cm) apart

Sweet potatoes can be a rewarding crop, but the vines are sensitive to frost and need 100 days of warmth, day and night, to crop well. However, provide them with a little attention, and you can still grow sweet potatoes in large containers or in raised beds under a plastic sheet with a floating row cover on top.

Order cuttings, known as "slips," or pot-grown young plants from mail order suppliers. 'Beauregard Improved' (105 days) is a high-yielding variety with orange flesh that is attractive and tasty. 'Georgia Jet' (90 days) is recommended for cool areas,

Leaves sprout from the sweet potato cuttings, and they will eventually form a mat of leaves as the vines spread and climb.

and 'Vardaman' (110 days) has shorter vines suitable for containers.

Planting

In warm areas, plant rooted slips right away in a light, free-draining potting mix or soil, with the first leaves level with the mix. In cold areas, start them in pots indoors in a warm, well-lit place. Transplant them into larger pots regularly, so they don't become root-bound.

Care

The vines spread and root as they grow to form a mat; provide supports and they will climb up and the tubers will be bigger. Pests, such as slugs and sweet potato weevils, can ruin tubers in raised beds; use organic slug pellets, if necessary. Flea beetles can attack the foliage; cover the plants with a fine mesh floating row cover.

Harvesting

Once the first fall frost blackens the tops, turn the tubers out of their pots, or remove the plastic from a raised bed and dig up the tubers. You can store any surplus, but first let the tubers dry in the sun for a day to cure the skin. Wrap each tuber in newspaper and store in a cool but frost-free, dry place.

Onions & Shallots

Take a shortcut by purchasing "sets," and you will have a supply of onions and shallots for storing. Or with just a little more effort, you can enjoy a fresh supply of scallions.

In early summer, shallots provide fresh green leaves as a foil to alyssum. In time, the tops will dry out and the bulbs will form at the base of the plants.

Getting started

What to plant Sets (immature bulbs)
Site Sunny; moist but well-drained potting mix
When Plant in spring (March–April) or fall, depending on variety
Container size Minimum of 18 inches (45 cm) in diameter
Spacing 3–4 inches (7.5–10 cm) apart

Onions and shallots are not the most ornamental crops and they dislike competition from other plants. However, you can tuck them into a corner out of view. An alternative is to grow scallions (see "Scallions" box, right) in small pots, and use them fresh, while still green. Choose long-day varieties if you live in the North; in the South, choose short-day varieties.

Planting

Push the onion or shallot sets into the surface of the potting mix so the tops are just buried, spacing them 3–4 inches (7.5–10 cm) apart. If you have leftover sets, you can plant them close together in a small container and cut the young shoots to use as scallions.

Care

Onions and shallots do not need much watering, and they do not need fertilizing. Be sure you do not overcrowd them.

Harvesting

For storing, wait until the tops of the onions or shallots are brown and dry, then move them somewhere protected from rain for the bulbs to ripen and dry off. Trim off the leaves about 1 inch (2.5 cm) from the bulb and store the bulbs in a cool, dry place.

Scallions

You can grow these thin onions in pots at any time and use them fresh (they will keep in the refrigerator for a few days but otherwise do not store well). Scatter the seeds thinly over a 12-inch (30-cm)-diameter pot filled with potting mix and cover them with ½ inch (1 cm) of potting mix. Once the seedlings appear, thin the plants so there is a seedling every ½–1 inch (1–2.5 cm), using surplus seedlings as you would chives. Keep the soil moist and start to harvest plants as scallions when they are the thickness of a pencil. Sow a pot every month from March to July.

Radishes

These popular, colorful roots can be small enough to grow almost anywhere, even in shallow containers, such as window boxes, or to fill in gaps in larger containers.

The typical, small spring radishes will be ready for harvesting within weeks, and they have more of a peppery bite to their flavor than the long-root daikons.

Getting started

What to plant Seeds
Site Cool partial shade; rich moist potting mix
When Early spring to fall, sow little and often, every two weeks
Container size Any
Spacing Sow seeds sparingly and thin to 1 inch (2.5 cm) apart

Not only will radishes grow in a small pot, depending on the type, but they can also be an incredibly quick-and-easy crop to grow. In fact, the real challenge might be choosing the variety to grow—there are over 200 varieties to choose from in an array of colors, including red, white, purple, and mauve. The typical, round, red spring varieties, such as 'Cherry Belle' and 'Jolly', are the quickest to grow, needing only three to four weeks from sowing, but there are also long-root types, such as red 'French Breakfast'. 'Munchen Bier' is one grown for its edible seedpods.

Other long-root radishes include the long-season winter radishes, such as Asian daikons. These can have roots as long as 8 inches (20 cm), so they need deeper pots, and the larger roots need more time to grow—as much as 10 weeks.

Planting

Sow spring radishes thinly, about a seed for every 1 inch (2.5 cm). You can sow them in March into pots destined for tender crops and harvest before the tender vegetables are planted. Or, after harvesting a crop of peas or another early vegetable, firm down the potting mix and sow radish seeds into it. Sow small quantities every two weeks.

Winter radishes are different. Sow them once in midsummer and let them grow much larger to store and use in the winter. They can be used raw or cooked.

Care

The plants grow quickly, so there is little care necessary other than keeping the potting mix moist; there is no need to fertilize them. Flea beetles can attack the leaves, but the roots will still be edible.

Harvesting

Start pulling up the plants when the roots are 1 inch (2.5 cm) in diameter; if larger than 2 inches (5 cm), they will lose their hot crunch and become strong and pithy. If you forget to harvest the plants, they will flower and run to seed. You can use the pods to add a hot crunch to salads.

Corn

This plant's tall foliage brings a dramatic touch to containers and, although yields may be small, there's nothing as sweet as freshly picked corn.

Getting started

What to plant Seeds
Site Full sun; sheltered; sandy or well-drained potting mix
When Spring; plant outside after there is no danger of frost
Container size Mininum 18 inches (45 cm) in diameter and 12 inches (30 cm) deep
Spacing Plant 6 inches (15 cm) apart

Unusual and fun, corn looks great in a container, and has plenty of space at the base for low-growing plants. At the moment, you can get only two or three cobs from a large pot, but improvements are on their way. Seed companies are trying to produce varieties that will have high yields in containers, and one such variety is the supersweet 'Mirai 003Y'.

The Native American method for growing corn, beans, and squash in a mound can be adapted for a large planter with a bush bean plant or a compact squash.

There are different types of corn: heirloom for old-fashioned flavor; sugar-enhanced, supersweets, which retain their sweetness longer after harvest; and those with extratender skins. Be guided by which varieties perform well in your area, if you want cobs before the first frost.

Planting

Plant the seeds into a container of potting mix after all danger of frost has past. Corn needs 70–100 days of warm weather from sowing to harvest for ears to form. In areas with a short growing season, start the seeds in small, deep pots, then move the young plants to the final container.

Care

As the plants grow, mound up the soil around them to secure them in the pot. Water is critical as the tassels and ears form. Corn is pollinated by wind; you can assist by tapping the tassels at the top of the plants so they fall on the silks below.

Harvesting

Watch the silks at the end of the ears; when they turn brown and start to dry, the cobs

A tall corn plant, with a spiky tassel at top, provides a focal point among a lower planting of orange-blossom nasturtiums.

are ready to harvest. To check, peel back the leaves and pierce a kernel; if the juice looks milky, it is ready. Cut off the ear with pruners; do not pull it or the plant may be dislodged from the pot or damaged. Cook the corn immediately, before the sugars turn to starch. Some types have thin skins so you can eat them raw straight from the plant.

Swiss Chard

One of the most colorful and versatile edibles for containers of all sizes, Swiss chard is easy to grow and will stay fresh in its container until you are ready to eat the leaves and stems.

Getting started

What to plant Seeds
Site Sun or partial shade
When Sow in spring to summer
Container size Minimum 12 inches (30 cm) in diameter
Spacing Sow 2 inches (5 cm) apart, then thin

You can eat the baby leaves of Swiss chard raw, or let the plants grow to produce mature leaves for cooking as a spinach substitute. The colorful stems of mature

Spinach and orach

Baby spinach work well in a mesclun mix, but to grow plants to serve as a vegetable you need large quantities—its volume decreases dramatically when cooked—and you need to sow every two weeks because the plants bolt to seed quickly. You can try sowing batches in a large planter divided into three, sowing every few weeks.

Orach, or mountain spinach, is an alternative to spinach in warm summers because it doesn't become bitter if it bolts. There are green, white, and eye-catching red types that will do well in a large planter.

plants are also edible—slice them and use for stir-frying, steaming, or baking.

For baby leaves, grow Swiss chard with other mesclun ingredients. For larger plants, grow as a single subject, because their roots will fill the pot and need plenty of nutrients and water. The most colorful mixture of stems is 'Bright Lights' (60 days), but you can also get single color selections.

Planting

The "seeds" are really a dried fruit cluster with several seeds that will germinate in a clump. You can separate the seedlings or grow them as a clump. A 12-inch (30-cm)-diameter container will hold three, four, or five seed clusters spaced 2 inches (5 cm) apart. Cover with ½ inch (1 cm) of potting mix. You can also grow the seeds in seed-starting trays and move them to a final pot.

Care

To grow the plants beyond the baby-leaf stage, keep the potting mix moist and use a balanced all-purpose fertilizer to keep the

A rainbow of colorful stems and the crinkly texture of the leaves make Swiss chard 'Bright Lights' a good candidate for an attractive container planting.

leaves and stems tender. If the plants do not get enough water or nutrients, they will become stringy and tough. Look for slugs and snails hiding among the stems.

Harvesting

Once the plants are growing, pick or cut a few outer leaves and stems from each plant and let the rest continue to grow, or cut the whole plant off at the base, leaving a stump that sometimes regrows. The crinkled leaves can hold a lot of dust, so wash them well in cold water before cooking. The plants may overwinter, then bolt in the spring.

The Squash Family

Just a few plants will reward you with a plentiful supply of zucchini and other summer squash all summer long, and your crops will be younger and fresher than store-bought ones, too.

Getting started

What to plant Plants or seeds
Site Sun, shelter
When Plant outside in late spring, when there is no danger of frost
Container size Minimum 12 inches (30 cm) in diameter
Spacing About 18–24 inches (45–60 cm) apart, depending on the variety

Seed companies are now selecting summer squash varieties, including zucchini, with a compact growth habit that produce a crop quickly, which are ideal for growing in pots. Look for the yellow squash 'Buckingham' or 'Soleil' (75 days) and the green striped 'Bush Baby'; all three are recommended for planters and small spaces.

Planting

Zucchini and summer squash are frost sensitive and dislike wind and cold soil. Give the plants the best start by filling a large pot with potting mix, mounding it up in the center, and letting it warm in the sun. Harden off young plants (see page 107) and then plant into the mound; the plants may need a floating row cover for a few days. Plant two plants in each container, then cut out the weakest one later on.

Zucchini flowers

You can pick and eat the flowers—the ones to choose are the large male ones because the females turn into the fruit. The female flowers are recognizable by a small embryonic swelling at their base. Pick the flowers in the morning, when they are completely open, and keep cool. Inspect the flowers for insects before stuffing them or dipping them in batter and frying them.

The large seeds are easy to handle, sow them directly into planting mounds in early summer when the soil is at least 60°F (16°C). Push in three or four seeds, then later pull out the two weakest seedlings. In cold areas, start the seeds in 3 inch (7.5 cm) pots a month before the last frost date.

Care

Drip irrigation will help keep the potting mix moist; avoid getting water on the foliage or stems. The secret is to water just enough to keep the potting mix moist and as the plant grows increase the amount of water. Feeding with a tomato fertilizer as directed on the package will encourage fruits. Watch out for powdery mildew and rotting fruits; remove any affected leaves or fruits promptly. If yellow marks or streaks appear on the leaves, it's a virus. Remove and destroy the plant. Cover the plants with a floating row cover if the squash vine borer is a problem, but remove it when the blooms appear to allow pollination.

Harvesting

Start cutting zucchini when they are 6 inches (15 cm) long or, for round squash, 2–3 inches (5–7.5 cm) in diameter. Use a knife to cut the zucchini or other squash from the plant; wear gloves because the plants can be spiny.

Once the plants start to produce a crop, cut the zucchini daily to encourage extra flowers, and therefore zucchini, to form.

Summer vs. winter squash

You can grow other summer squash—such as patty pans, with their scalloped-edged flying-saucer shape (below)—in exactly the same way as zucchini, although the plants can be larger. All types of summer squash, including zucchini, are prolific croppers, but they all have soft skins that make them unsuitable for long-term storage. 'Summer Ball' (75–90 days), which has round, yellow fruits that can be cut young or left to ripen and stored for a short period, is suitable for growing in containers.

Conversely, winter squash, which includes pumpkins, have a hard, inedible rind, which means you can leave them in the sun to ripen and then store the fruits. Of the two, winter squash store well, but the plants need at least 10 square feet (1 m²) per plant, making them impractical for growing in pots. The exception are some acorn types that have a bushy habit, which you could try in a large container.

Tomatoes

From compact bushes to sprawling vines, there is no shortage of tomato types—and as long as you can find a sunny site, no matter how small it is, you can grow your own tomatoes.

Getting started

What to plant Plants
Site Full sun, sheltered; rich potting mix
When Late spring, plant outside after there is no danger of frost
Container size Varies greatly, but at least 8 inches (20 cm) in diameter
Spacing Varies, usually one plant per container

There are plenty of good trailing tomato varieties that are the perfect choice for growing in hanging baskets or for tumbling out of tall pots. In addition, plant breeders have been producing ultracompact varieties, such as 'Venus', that will fit in a window box or small 1-quart (1-liter) pot. At the other end of the spectrum, there are the vinelike indeterminate types that, if trained (see "Indeterminate support," above), will continue to provide a crop all season. A

new development for gardeners is "turbo" tomato plants, which are varieties grafted onto vigorous rootstock so the plants grow quicker and stronger with higher yields. Both of these more vigorous plants are best if you want to cook or preserve tomatoes.

Indeterminate support

An indeterminate variety will grow on and on as a single stem. Bring it under control by tying the main stem to a single wooden stake or a metal spiral support with plant ties. Remove any side shoots that emerge where the leaves join the main stem but leave the flower shoots. Remove lower leaves that turn yellow as growth continues.

Instead of sowing seeds, the simplest way to start is to choose two or three different young plants from a garden center in late spring. Wait until late spring to buy

Tomatoes come in an amazing array of sizes, shapes, and colors, and your choice may depend on how you want to eat the tomato. From left to right are a compact bush tomato producing medium tomatoes, tumbling tomatoes with tiny fruit, an indeterminate plant that will provide a long supply of larger tomatoes, and one of the varieties that produce elongated tomatoes. Whatever type they are, harvest the tomatoes a day or two early, before their skins split.

bushy, healthy green plants. If you buy them too early, you will have to keep them in a light, frost-free place and they quickly outgrow their pots. However, if you wait too long, the plants may be starved (with purple tinges to foliage) and straggling.

Planting

Plant standard bush, dwarf, or patio plants sold in 3-inch (7.5-cm) pots straight into 12–14-inch (30–35 cm)-diameter hanging baskets or other containers with a capacity of at least 3 gallons (11 liters). The ultracompact ones need an area of

6–8 inches (15–20 cm) to themselves, but you can make them part of a mixed basket if there is a large volume of potting mix to retain moisture. If there is a delay in planting in the final container, pot the plants into the next size pot or fertilize them.

Care

Water the plants regularly—an automatic-drip irrigation system is a boon here—and once the plants are established, give them a tomato fertilizer following the package directions. If you fertilize your tomatoes regularly, you could have three times the

crop compared to unfed plants. Provide indeterminate types with support.

Harvesting

Pick tomatoes when the skin has reached its mature color. This is easy to determine in red, orange, and brown varieties, but it is tricky for yellows and whites, so just taste these. Pick before they turn soft or the skin splits because they will quickly rot. It is better to pick them a bit unripe and put them on a sunny windowsill to ripen. Aim to pick all the tomatoes as they ripen, because ripe fruit will rot and drop onto the ground.

Basil

Pretty, neat, and tasty, a selection of different basil varieties will be perfect for tabletop flowerpots and tidy enough for window boxes, too.

When basil plants are young, take only a few leaves from each plant. You can use these fresh in salads or for topping a pizza straight out of the oven.

Getting started

What to plant Plants or seeds
Site Warm and sunny; they are frost sensitive
When Sow in midspring, then little and often, every two weeks
Container size 6 inches (15 cm) in diameter
Spacing 6 inches (15 cm) apart

There is a huge range of popular basil varieties that look as good as they taste, including ones with different textures, sizes, and foliage color. Large-leaved basil plants provide leaves in quantity, which is ideal for making pesto. Opt for the classic bush basil or 'Sweet Genovese', which have a strong aroma and are easy to find. Others you might come across are 'Puck', with a neat habit, 'Green Ruffles', which has pale green leaves, and 'Lettuce-leaved'.

Another good ornamental basil is 'Magical Michael', with a neat habit, dark stems, and purple flowers. For dark purple foliage, there is 'Purple Ruffles'; the plant is especially colorful when the lilac-pink flowers are out. There are also the Greek and Thai types (see "Greek or Thai," left).

Greek or Thai

Basil is popular around the world. 'Aristotle' is a small-leaved Greek basil that grows to only 8 inches (20 cm) high but can spread to 16 inches (40 cm); you can trim it to shape. The flavor is mild but you can use sprigs of whole leaves for a garnish.

For a spicy aroma and aniseed flavor, try Thai basil 'Siam Queen', and use it in stir-fries or Asian dishes. 'Christmas Basil' is a Thai basil with a high oil content (a sign of a great pesto ingredient) but just as important, it is a neat, attractive plant.

Planting

Basil plants are sensitive to frost and cold, damp conditions, so wait to buy plants in early summer. Keep the pots raised up on tabletops, shelves, and window boxes for extra warmth.

Alternatively, sow seeds in pots from midspring (early April) onward in a light, warm (at least 65°F/18°C) location, such as a heated propagator in a greenhouse or on the kitchen windowsill. Sow three to four seeds in a 3-inch (7.5-cm) pot to keep root disturbance to a minimum. Keep the potting mix on the dry side.

Care

Pinch off the growing tips when the plants are 6 inches (15 cm) tall. Protect from slugs and snails. Move them outside once the risk of frost has passed. Pinch off the flower buds to encourage the plant to remain bushy. Keep the potting mix on the dry side to avoid root rots and diseases.

Harvesting

Use as needed, picking a few leaves from each plant. Before the first frost arrives, when the plants will die, harvest all the leaves; freeze whole in small plastic bags.

Chives

A great little herb for beginners, chives are easy to grow and will come back year after year. Not only are the leaves suitable for eating, but the attractive flowers are edible, too.

Getting started

What to plant Plants or seeds
Site Any sun or partial shade, moist or dry
When Sow seeds in spring
Container size 6 inches (15 cm) in diameter
Spacing Plants should be 6 inches (15 cm) apart

This pretty, hardy perennial, with its thin, hollow leaves and small mauve flowers, will fit into any space. There is also a white-flowered form, but it is less widely available. Another alternative is the garlic chive (also known as Chinese chive); it has a mild garlic flavor, flatter leaves, and white flowers.

When the flowers appear in early summer, you can use the petals to sprinkle over a salad.

The leaves have a mild onion flavor that is suitable for soups, salads, and other dishes.

Planting

Once the temperature reaches 68°F (20°C) in spring, you can sow three to four seeds ¾ inch (2 cm) deep in small pots. Thin out the young plants to leave the strongest seedling. Chives will fit into mixed herb plantings in pots, or you can keep three small pots with chives growing at different harvesting stages. To keep chive plants going year after year, grow them in a soil-based potting mix.

Care

Chives need little care. The plants self-seed easily, so you may find new seedlings growing near mature plants. The plants are perennials that die down in winter, and they should be cut back to near potting mix level. When a clump outgrows a pot, you can remove and split it, then replant healthy sections of the clump. Divide the clumps every three years to help prevent them from developing rust, which occurs if they become overcrowded.

Harvesting

Chives have hollow stems that grow from the base, so it is easy to use a pair of scissors to snip them. Cut the stems ½ inch (1 cm) from the base; if you just snip the tips, they turn brown and look unsightly. When the leaves are green and fresh in summer, harvest enough to freeze for use in winter. Freeze snipped chives on a cookie sheet, then transfer to a container.

Coriander & Cilantro

There are coriander varieties that continue to produce plenty of leaves, which we call cilantro, even when the plants are cut back, so even the smallest pot can supply plenty of cilantro.

Getting started

What to plant Seeds
Site Sun or partial shade for leaves; well-drained potting mix
When Sow in midspring (April–May), every four weeks until July
Container size Minimum 6 inches (15 cm) in diameter
Spacing 6–8 inches (15–20 cm) apart

Choose coriander varieties that are geared to either leaf production or seed production. You can grow some newer varieties, such as 'Calypso', as part of a mesclun mix (see pages 126–127) because it is slow to set seed and its growing points are close to the ground. This means that just one sowing can be cut down and will grow again three to five times if the potting mix is kept moist. Another slow-to-bolt variety is 'Confetti', which has fine feathery leaves that are useful as a garnish.

For seed production, look for the fast-growing Moroccan coriander. Make one sowing in May, then harvest the seeds in August.

Planting

Sow seeds directly into their final pots. The seeds are large and easy to handle, so push them ¼ inch

The whole coriander plant is edible—the leaves, stems, seeds, and even the roots, which are popular in Thai cooking.

(5 mm) down into the potting mix. Space the seeds 1 inch (2.5 cm) apart if you are growing them for their the leaves; otherwise thin the plants to 6–8 inches (15–20 cm). You can sow leafy varieties all year round and keep them in a pot on a windowsill.

Care

Plants need little aftercare; just keep the potting medium moist.

Harvesting

Cut the leaves with a pair of scissors when the plants are 4 inches (10 cm) high, cutting back to 1–2 inches (2.5–5 cm) from the ground. If you have a cut-and-come-again variety, such as 'Calypso', repeat the harvesting every month or so. Coriander grows quickly, and it matures rapidly beyond being usable in the kitchen, so freeze batches in ice-cube trays in early summer. In most areas, it is difficult to grow in fall and winter, so if you want fresh leaves in winter, grow indoors on a windowsill.

Harvest the roots before the plant runs to seed. Use them to flavor soups, such as carrot soup, and in curries.

Collect the seeds in late summer, when they turn pale brown. To collect them, cut the stalks and put them in a paper bag. The seeds will drop out into the bag after two weeks. When dry, store them in screw-top jars in a cool, dark place.

Dill

Its feathery foliage and bright green-yellow flowers make dill an attractive container plant whose leaves and seeds are used in dips, pickles, and preserves.

Dill leaves have more flavor before the plant flowers, so pinch off flower stalks if you don't want seeds.

Getting started

What to plant Seed or plants
Site Full sun; well-drained potting mix
When Sow seeds in late spring (April) and every month until June
Container size Minimum 6 inches (15 cm) in diameter
Spacing Thin out seedlings to 4–6 inches (10–15 cm) apart

If you want seeds, try 'Mammoth', but most varieties run to seed quickly if their leaves are not harvested. 'Fernleaf' is popular.

Planting

The plants don't like disturbance, so sow the seeds in their final pot or buy young plants.

Care

At first let the mix dry out a little between watering; as they mature, keep the potting mix moist.

Harvesting

Cut the leaves once the dill starts growing.

Fennel

A tall herb plant that has green or bronze feathery foliage with an anise flavor, fennel can grow in a large, deep planter or a raised bed.

Fennel is an attractive plant to grow with other herbs and flowers in late spring to midsummer.

Getting started

What to plant One plant
Site Sun in fertile potting mix
When Plant in spring
Container size 24 inches (60 cm) in diameter
Spacing 20–24 inches (50–60 cm)

A single fennel plant will provide a mass of leaves, so it is suitable for a small site.

Planting

Plant in spring; the plant has a long taproot, so grow it in a large, deep pot. Fennel can reach 5 feet (1.5 m) high in a border, but its growth is less in a container. Be aware: If left to flower, the plant will self-seed. Do not plant near dill to prevent cross-pollination.

Care

If you make sure the taproot has room to grow and keep the potting mix moist, the plant will thrive. Fennel dies back in winter.

Harvesting

Cut the foliage as required; the stems and flowers can be added to pickles or salads.

Edible Flowers

Enjoy the beauty of edible flowers while they are growing alongside vegetables and mesclun mixes in containers, then pick a few to add color to homegrown salads.

Getting started

What to plant Seeds or plants
Site Sun or partial shade
When Sow seeds in early spring or buy young plants in late spring to early summer
Container size 12 inches (30 cm) in diameter
Spacing 6 inches (15 cm) apart

If you plan to add flower petals to food, besides making sure they are insect free, use only flowers that have not been sprayed with chemicals. To be sure of what you are eating, either buy organically grown plants or raise your own plants from seeds.

Planting

Depending on the flowers, add them to a group planting with other plants requiring similar growing conditions or plant them later to fill a gap once a vegetable has been harvested. Nasturtiums have large seeds that you can push ½ inch (1 cm) down into the potting mix when planting hanging baskets and window boxes.

Care

Annual flowers growing alongside lettuce and mesclun, herbs, and vegetables in containers need little extra care. Remove

any diseased leaves, and remove faded flowers promptly so more will produce.

Harvesting

Pick the flowers early in the morning, once the dew has dried. There is no need to wash them, but check for insects inside. Place the stems in a jar of cold water, or put the flowers in a plastic bag and store it in the refrigerator.

From pastel roses, cheerful violas, bright nasturtiums to dainty borage, popular marigold, and fragrant lavender (left to right), there's plenty to choose from when growing edible flowers. The center of a flower can be bitter, so use only the petals.

A selection of annual flowers

Not all flowers are edible, but the following flowers are safe to eat. (For roses and lavender, see page 50.) Because flowers can share the same common name, even if they are of different species, use the botanical names given below when purchasing seeds.

Nasturtiums *(Tropaeolum majus)* These have a distinct peppery taste, and there are a lot of different varieties to choose from, ranging from orange and red to cream flowers; some are trailing plants, while others are bushy. Nasturtiums are easy to grow in hot, dry sites, but they can be a magnet for pests.

Calendula The original pot marigold *(Calendula officinalis)* was bright orange, but there are now variations, such as apricot shades, mahogany red, and double flowers. The petals have a slight nutty taste; chopped petals add a golden color to rice or butter.

Violas and violets All violas are edible and have small pretty flowers that tolerate shade. The sweet violets *(Viola odorata)* have the best flavor; this is a hardy perennial plant.

Borage The blue petals of *Borago officinalis* have a cucumber flavor and look pretty floating in summer drinks or added to ice cubes. The plant tolerates some shade and dry conditions.

Garlic

You may never need to buy garlic again if you grow your own, because cloves divide and produce more and more bulbs. Garlic takes up little space, and it is easy to grow and store.

Garlic reproduces by dividing and some no longer flower, but there are many varieties available.

Getting started

What to plant Certified bulbs
Site Sun in moist but well-drained potting mix
When Plant in spring or fall, depending on variety
Container size 12 inches (30 cm) in diameter
Spacing 6 inches (15 cm) for bulbs (less if growing for only leaves)

Buy certified garlic bulbs from a garden center or specialty supplier instead of using garlic from a grocery store. They are produced under controlled conditions so there is less risk of plant viruses, and they are not treated to prevent them from sprouting. A mail-order supplier will have a range of varieties to choose from.

Garlic is divided into two types. Hardneck (rocambole) types have a twisting central shoot that hardens in late summer with the cloves forming around it. Hardneck varieties do well in cold areas and have a strong flavor, but they do not store well. If you live in a warm area, you can choose softneck varieties, which have a bulb with several layers of overlapping cloves, like an artichoke; these store well.

Planting

Remove the papery skin and separate the bulb into cloves. Plant each one upright, with the flat base of the clove pointing down. Push down so the tops are just covered. Birds pull out the cloves, so protect them with a net cover until the shoots form.

Care

Once planted, the garlic needs little care, but it does not like to be crowded by other plants. Keep the potting mix moist in dry spells. Plants may run to seed and produce a long flower stalk or "scape"; there may still be a crop at the base but it will not store as well. You can cut up the scapes and use them to flavor dishes. When the tops of the leaves start to dry off, pull back the potting mix to expose the bulb so it can cure.

Harvesting

Dry the bulbs in the sun or, if rain is due, move then to dry indoors on a sunny windowsill. Rub any dry potting mix off the bulbs and store them in a dry and cool but frost-free location—a kitchen is often not the best place because it is too humid.

If you have a lot of bulbs (at least nine) with long lengths of dead leaves attached, you can make a garlic braid to hang up on a hook in a garage. Start with three bulbs, then add three more at a time, braiding the dead leaves as you go. At the end, loop the dead leaves over and tie in place so you can hang up the braid.

Using extra garlic

If you have more garlic cloves than you need for growing garlic, they still serve a purpose. Plant them in small pots of potting mix, then harvest the green shoots to use as a substitute for chives. You can also plant whole bulbs of garlic to produce a large clump of green shoots.

Marjoram & Oregano

Both marjoram and oregano are Mediterranean plants, often used as a flavoring in dishes from that region. These trouble-free plants produce flowers loved by butterflies and bees.

Getting started

What to plant Plants
Site Warm, sunny, in well-drained potting mix
When Plant in late spring
Container size Varies, but at least 12 inches (30 cm) in diameter
Spacing 6–12 inches (15–30 cm) apart

To get the intense flavor from the leaves, these plants need warm, dry conditions. In addition to sweet marjoram *(Origanum majorana)* and oregano *(O. vulgare),* you might also come across pot marjoram *(O. onites),* a low-spreading perennial that is useful for containers. Greek oregano is a

Grow sweet marjoram as an annual herb for its delicate, aromatic leaves. Grow it alone or combine it with another herb, such as thyme.

type of *O. vulgare* that has a more pungent aroma but is less hardy. If in doubt, rub a leaf between finger and thumb to check the aroma. There are golden or yellow-leaved forms that look attractive.

Planting

You can plant hardy species in the spring, but first harden them off if they have been indoors. For tender types, wait until after the last frost. To grow perennials, use a soil-based mix with sand to improve drainage.

Care

To encourage bushy growth, pinch off the shoot tips. Oregano is a vigorous perennial; when it is too large for the pot, divide the clump and replant healthy young sections.

Harvesting

Pick leaves as soon as the plant is growing well. Cut the plants back to the base several times during the growing season. They will grow again, so even a single plant will yield enough leaves for drying.

The leaves of oregano are at their best in the warmer months, which is the best time for harvesting.

Drying herbs in a microwave

The dried leaves of marjoram and oregano have a more intense aroma than fresh leaves. You can hang them up in a well-ventilated place for a week or speed up the pace by using a microwave. Microwave drying works best in small batches—a few handfuls of leaves at a time. Remove any diseased or dead leaves, then wash the herbs in cold water and pat dry between paper towels. Scatter the leaves in a single layer over two sheets of paper towel and microwave for 2 minutes. They should be brittle but still green; if not, microwave again for 30–60 seconds. Crumble the leaves between finger and thumb and store in a clean screw-top jar. Label with the herb name and date and use within six months.

Mint

From sauces to teas, mint is a popular herb in the kitchen. The plants are hardy and easy to grow, but there is a knack to keeping up a regular supply of healthy leaves.

Getting started

What to plant Plants
Site Some sun or partial shade
When Plant in spring
Container size Minimum 14 inches (35 cm) in diameter
Spacing Minimum 18 inches (45 cm)

Mints come in a huge array with a wide range of flavors, from spearmint and peppermint to pineapple mint, as well as different leaf textures, such as the large, soft leaves of 'Apple Mint' and the crinkly leaves of 'Curly'.

Mint plants are hardy and spread through the soil by vigorous underground stems, so they soon swamp other herbs. Even if you buy a container of mixed herbs, replant mint into its own container as soon as possible. An alternative to a pot is to sink a bottomless bucket into the ground with 2–4 inches (5–10 cm) above ground, which reduces the need for watering; you will still need to replant it in two to three years.

Planting

Plant a small started plant in the center of a container and water it well. Mint is often one of the first herbs to be available, so you can plant it in early spring (April).

The secret to successfully growing mint is to remember that it is not a Mediterranean herb; mint thrives in moist potting mix and partial shade.

Care

During the growing season, the plant will spread to the edge of the pot and start to fill it. If it runs out of moisture or nutrients, the middle of the plant will die and the young shoots at the edges will be starved and prone to disease, such as rust or powdery mildew. Keep your mint fresh by using a large pot and keeping it moist. Move young runners into pots of fresh potting mix or give the plants a balanced all-purpose fertilizer. Dispose of any diseased or old plant debris.

The flowers are pretty and are often visited by bees and butterflies, but the seedlings can be a nuisance, even in a pot. Seedlings do not grow like their parent plant and can take over, so pull up any you see.

Harvesting

Mints are perennial plants, but the leaves are at their peak for harvesting from early summer to early fall. First, pinch off 1 inch (2.5 cm) of the growing tips for use, which will also help the plant to bush out. Later, harvest regularly. When you want to dry a large quantity (see "Drying herbs in a microwave," page 149) or make a batch of mint sauce, cut the plants down to the base. For fresh mint in winter, dig up runners in fall and lay them flat in a pot filled halfway with potting mix. Add a thin layer of potting mix over them and keep on a windowsill.

Parsley

Both flat-leaf Italian parsley and curly parsley are essential herbs. They are tolerant plants that offer regular handfuls of leaves for use raw as a garnish and cooked in sauces.

Flat-leaf Italian parsley has leaves that look similar to cilantro, but they have the same flavor as curly parsley.

Getting started

What to plant Seeds
Site Sun or partial shade, moist potting mix
When Sow seeds in spring to early summer (March to June); sow batches every three months
Container size 6 inches (15 cm) in diameter
Spacing 6 inches (15 cm)

Parsley tolerates some shade and is reasonably hardy, so even a small space can supply fresh leaves for most of the year. The plant is actually a biennial, forming leaves the first year, flowering, then dying in its second year. In practice, however, it is easiest to grow parsley as an annual.

Curly parsley has a wonderful fluffy texture and an intense green color that looks great in a mixed planting with bright flowers. Flat-leaf Italian parsley is often recommended by chefs for its flavor and is used in salads.

The advantage of growing either type of parsley in pots instead of in the garden is that late and early pickings are less likely to be splashed with mud and soil, which is hard to clean from the leaves. Alternatively,

to keep the leaves cleaner, you can opt for a variety with longer stems, such as 'Giant Italian Oscar'; this is a vigorous variety that is a good choice for raised beds. At the other extreme, compact varieties, such as 'Laura', suit window boxes.

Planting

For regular quantities, grow parsley from seeds. Buy a fresh packet of seeds each year. Sprinkle them on the surface of the potting mix in the final container (parsley doesn't transplant well) and lightly cover with the mix. Keep at 60°F (16°C) and keep the potting mix moist until the seeds germinate. You can harvest the seedlings early and add to salads or thin out the seedlings to 1 inch (2.5 cm) apart and grow them as larger plants.

Care

Keep the potting mix moist and watch out for slugs and carrot rust fly; if the latter attacks the roots, the foliage will turn reddish. Parsley likes partial shade

in summer. In warm climates, outdoor sowings do well in winter; a crop cover improves the leaf quality. In cold climates, move the pot indoors to a sunny windowsill.

Harvesting

Cut the plants with a pair of scissors as needed. The stems add plenty of flavor to stocks; however, they are tough to eat raw, so for salads only snip off the leaves. Surplus parsley freezes well, either chopped and frozen in ice-cube trays with a little water, or cut the stems and leaves and freeze in plastic bags.

Rosemary

An aromatic, evergreen shrub with flavorful, needlelike leaves and attractive small flowers, rosemary is a tender plant that is more suitable for growing in containers in cold areas.

Getting started

What to plant Plants
Site Sun and shelter in a well-drained potting mix
When Spring or summer
Container size Minimum 8 inches (20 cm) in diameter
Spacing Minimum 8 inches (20 cm)

If you keep a young rosemary plant clipped to keep it within bounds, you can partner it with a flowering plant—but make sure its partner prefers dry soil.

Originally a Mediterranean shrub, rosemary has long been cultivated in Europe and North America as a garden plant. It offers white or pale lavender-blue flowers in late spring. Plants can die in winter because they dislike cold, wet soil. However, in the right conditions, such as a container with plenty of drainage and a soil-based potting mix plus a couple of handfuls of sand, it can survive in warm areas.

For containers, a young bushy plant or a prostrate form that is less than 6 inches (15 cm) high but grows sideways like a mat are two budget options. You can grow a prostrate rosemary in a hanging basket and move it into a porch or sunroom over winter. More stylish, perhaps, is to train a rosemary on a long stem as a mini-standard, with the leaves growing above a main stem. If you grow rosemary in this way, plant different herbs underneath for an attractive planting to display by a front door.

There are named varieties, such as 'Arp', which has better winter hardiness than most, and 'Severn Sea', which has light blue flowers and makes a 3-foot (90-cm) mound of arching stems.

Planting

Start with a healthy, young plant in spring and plant it into its final container. Keep the plant watered until it is growing well, then ease off so the potting mix is barely damp.

Care

Clip the plant after flowering to shape it or let it sprawl. Pinch off the tips to encourage bushy growth. In most regions, rosemary won't survive the winter unless you bring the pot indoors and keep it by a sunny windowsill. In case the plant doesn't last, take a few 4-inch (10-cm) cuttings in summer and plant in a damp potting mix.

Harvesting

Rosemary has a strong flavor so only small quantities of leaves are needed. Start picking needles as soon as the plant is growing well. Use sprigs whole when roasting meat and remove them before serving, or strip the needles from the stems and finely chop to add to dishes. Once the stems harden, you can cut long lengths, strip them of their needles except for the tips, and use as kabob sticks.

Sage

The leaves of this attractive Mediterranean shrub have a strong, pungent aroma, so one or two small, young sage plants should supply you with enough leaves for the kitchen.

The textured leaves of sage make it an attractive plant, especially those with variegated colors, such as this green-and-cream specimen.

Getting started

What to plant Plants
Site Warm, sunny, and well-drained potting mix
When Plant in spring or summer
Container size 8 inches (20 cm) in diameter
Spacing 12 inches (30 cm)

Because sage plants have attractive, long-lasting foliage, they work well in mixed plantings. The common sage (Salvia officinalis) is a woody plant with plain green leaves, and these leaves are the traditional ones used in cooking. There are varieties with colorful foliage, however, that are more ornamental for containers, and these have enough aroma in the leaves to be good substitutes. There are three varieties that particularly earn their keep. 'Icterina', with yellow-and-green variegated foliage, looks cheerful when paired with yellow flowers or planted in light blue or black containers. 'Tricolor' has green-and-cream variegated leaves flecked with pink that looks great teamed with pink, whether you choose pink flowers or pink pots. 'Purpuracens', with brooding, dark purple leaves, is a perfect foil for pink roses or silver containers.

Other culinary sages

The salvia family offers a few other sage plants that have culinary uses. Use clary (Salvia sclarea), a biennial with heart-shaped leaves, like common sage. Or for something different, try pineapple sage (S. elegans or S. rutilans), with aromatic leaves that smell like pineapple. Greek sage (S. fruticosa or S. triloba) is the sage typically sold in supermarkets, but it lacks the flavor of common sage.

Planting

Buy young sage plants in 3-inch (7.5 cm) pots or take 6-inch (15-cm) cuttings from already existing sage plants—your own or from a neighbor or friend—if you have somewhere to overwinter them. Plant them in a seed-starting mix after treating the cut ends with a root-inducing hormone powder, then move them into large pots in spring or summer. If you want to keep the plants for a few years before they get too woody, plant them in a soil-based potting mix.

Care

Aftercare is minimal; sage is drought tolerant and needs no fertilizing.

Harvesting

Sage has a strong flavor, so use it sparingly, picking only a few leaves as required. The foliage will die back in winter except for in warm climates, so pick and preserve batches of leaves in the summer.

To make sage butter, chop fresh sage and mix it with butter before freezing for up to two months. Dry sage by spreading out the leaves in a single layer to dry in the sun or use a microwave (see "Drying herbs in a microwave," page 149). Crumble the dried leaves into jars for storing.

Tarragon

Just a few leaves will add a delicate but warm anise flavor to chicken and fish dishes, so it is well worth adding a tarragon plant to your herb collection.

Warm weather substitute

If you live in a warm climate where French tarragon struggles, try Mexican tarragon *(Tagetes lucida),* also known as pericon or sweet-scented marigold. Grow it as an annual, sowing seeds indoors two months before the last spring frost. Harden off the seedlings before moving it outdoors, and enjoy the leaves in tea and as an herb.

You can grow tarragon on its own, but it is also the perfect partner for other perennial herbs that prefer dry soil, such as savory or thyme.

Getting started

What to plant Plants
Site Warm, sun, and in well-drained potting mix
When Plant in late spring to early summer
Container size Minimum 12 inches (30 cm) in diameter
Spacing 12 inches (30 cm)

Tarragon is an unobtrusive, hardy perennial, with a clump of narrow leaves that rarely flowers. It does best in cool summers; however, it is easy to lose it during winter in cold, wet soil, so it is a good choice for growing in containers, where it does well.

When buying tarragon to use in the kitchen, choose French tarragon *(Artemisia dracunculus* var. *sativa).* Its long, thin leaves have the best flavor. To make sure you are not buying Russian tarragon *(A. dracunculus* ssp. *dracunculoides),* taste a leaf before buying a plant; the leaves of Russian tarragon have a more bitter taste.

Planting

Wait until late spring to early summer before buying a plant, then choose one with some new growth you can taste. Plant into a pot filled with a soil-based potting mix with some sand, and put it in a warm sunny spot. Pair it with ornamentals but nothing vigorous because it easily gets swamped.

Care

Water the potting mix until the plant grows well, then it is tolerant to drought. The plant growth may slow down, and then start again in fall. When the top growth dies down, cut away the debris and protect the plant's crown with a mulch, such as bark chips. Move the pot indoors in winter or insulate the pot with a double layer of bubble wrap. Buy a new plant every few years.

Harvesting

The harvest period is short (midsummer to early fall), so pinch off the growing tips for kitchen use as soon as the plant is growing. Freeze any surplus or add a sprig to a bottle of vinegar and use in salad dressings.

Thyme

A group of low-growing, pretty herbs with aromatic leaves, thymes thrive in all types of containers, from hanging baskets to shallow pans to pots.

Getting started

What to plant Plants
Site Sun, in a well-drained potting mix
When Plant in spring
Container size 6 inches (15 cm) in diameter
Spacing 8 inches (20 cm), but varies, depending on the variety

All thyme plants are woody perennial plants, which means the pungent leaves are available most of the year for cooking. To get the most out of these plants, grow thyme plants in containers to keep the leaves clean of mud and debris and put them near the kitchen door.

New plants from old

To propagate, or grow new perennials from old ones, divide a clump in spring or fall (preserving as much of the roots as you can) and plant new healthy growth. Or take 6-inch (15-cm) cuttings in spring or early summer, treat them with a root-inducing hormone powder (sold in garden centers), and let them root in wet sand for two to three weeks before replanting.

There is a huge range of thyme plants, and it is fun to have a collection for a variety of flavors to use in the kitchen. The best known for cooking is common thyme *(Thymus vulgaris),* which forms an upright bush with mauve-pink flowers in summer. Those with variegated leaves add interest, either splashed with golden yellow or silver-gray ('Silver Needle'), whereas others *(T. × citriodorus)* have a lemon flavor. In general, the flowers are pretty pink, white, or lilac and are loved by bees.

Planting

Thyme plants are one of the few plants that thrive in shallow baskets or wall planters, but they do like coarse drainage. A group of thymes works well together but, if growing them with other plants, make sure they are not overtaken by their partners and that the potting mix is not too wet.

Care

Water the plants when young, but thereafter just keep the potting mix on the dry side.

Thyme plants are small and take up little space, so it is easy to have just a single pot of thyme for a fresh supply of leaves.

Trim plants after flowering to improve their shape and remove any dead stems. You can take cuttings every three or four years to rejuvenate a plant if it starts to get leggy or bare in the center.

Harvesting

Cut the stems as needed. The leaves pick up dust, so wash the stems after picking, then pick the tiny leaves off in the kitchen. You can pick the leaves fresh all winter in warm climates, but it is easier to harvest and dry surplus leaves in summer before the plants flower. Dry in a microwave (see "Drying herbs in a microwave," page 149).

Strawberries

The aroma and taste of fresh homegrown strawberries is far superior to any store-bought offerings, and using containers simplifies the growing of this quick-growing fruit.

Getting started

What to plant Plants
Site Full sun, potting mix
When Buy started plants in spring or use rooted runners in early fall
Container size Minimum 12 inches (30 cm) in diameter
Spacing Plant 5–6 inches (12.5–15 cm) apart

There are some advantages to growing strawberries in containers instead of in the ground. First, there is no need to keep moving the strawberry bed around the yard every three years to prevent a buildup of soil-borne diseases. The berries are held off the ground so they are cleaner and you can grow the strawberries in a raised location, which makes them easier to pick without bending down.

Strawberry plants will last three years if you use a durable container full of a soil-based potting mix and if you can protect the containers over winter in cold areas.

Fresh strawberries are attractive, but they will also attract animals, such as birds. Protect the plants with a netting to help keep the animals at bay.

Otherwise, grow the plants for only one year, in which case any potting mix will do.

There are June-bearing varieties that will provide a bumper crop, as well as everbearing varieties that produce fewer berries but over a longer season. Growing three to five of each in their own container will spread the cropping season; however, you have room for only one variety, make it an early June-bearing strawberry.

Another benefit of growing strawberries in lightweight pots is that you can extend their growing season. The trick is to move the pots under cover into a plastic tunnel or greenhouse over winter, where they will flower up to three weeks earlier than those growing outside. So even if you grow only one variety, having a couple of pots means you can encourage one to fruit earlier than the other.

Planting

After a few years, strawberry plants tend to become infected with plant viruses, so instead of accepting free runners from a neighbor or friend, it is best to order guaranteed virus-free plants from a reliable garden fruit supplier in spring.

On arrival the plants look dry and dormant, but they will quickly revive after the roots are well watered, and they will grow rapidly. Immediately plant the strawberries into individual pots, insulate the pots for over winter, then replant the best into their final pot in spring. The top of the plant's crown should be just above soil level.

Strawberry plants are short, although the fruiting stems can be long, so hanging baskets, as well as tall pots, are suitable containers for growing them.

Container options

Flowerpots The basic terra-cotta flowerpot works well if you have room for five or six, along a wall or up steps, for example. Allow for one plant per 6-inch (15-cm)-diameter pot. With smaller pots, you can move them more easily, for example, to bring them indoors to a bright windowsill instead of covering with netting when the berries are ripe.

Hanging basket A 12-inch (30-cm)-diameter hanging basket will hold three strawberry plants with room to sink in an empty plant pot to help direct water into the potting mix. They will need to be netted against birds, but the netting can be easily attached to the wall bracket.

Planting bags Woven plastic strawberry bags are similar to potato bags but with planting pockets. They are inexpensive and safe for children to use because they can drag them around using the handles. Being a flexible material, the potting mix tends to separate from the planter, so it needs to be refirmed before watering or the water will run down the inside wall.

Strawberry pot Designed to hold about 12 plants in planting pockets around the sides of the pot as well as at the top, these are difficult to plant and water and can be heavy, but they save on space.

Care

During the first watering, apply it gently, using a rose attachment on the watering can to break up the water into drops. Firm in the potting mix and adjust the planting, if necessary. Keep the potting mix moist but not waterlogged and apply a tomato fertilizer as the fruit form. When the fruit start to swell, cover the pot with netting, making sure it sits away from the berries, to prevent birds from pecking them.

If strawberries are planted on all sides of the container, rotate the pot to encourage even growth and ripening. Slugs and snails will eat the fruit; if they can reach a container, apply a copper band around the upper section of the pot (see pages 110–111).

To maintain the strength of the original strawberry plants, remove runners from the parent plants—it keeps the planting neater, too. Cut off the unhealthy-looking leaves from the parent plant to reduce the risk of disease. Replace the plants and potting mix after two to three years or sooner if the foliage has yellow streaks and mottling.

Harvesting

You can pick fruit in the first summer after planting, but the yields can be more than double in the second year. Pick the ripe fruit every day or two; ripe fruit quickly spoils. Pick with the green stem intact, wash the fruit gently, and then remove the stem.

Index

Photo Credits

Abbreviations: T = Top;
M = Middle; B = Bottom;
L = Left; R = Right
Front Cover: GAP: Graham Strong (TL).
Friedrich Strauss (BL). Photolibrary:
Gary K. Smith (TR). Mark Winwood:
(ML).
Back Cover: Mark Winwood.
Alamy: Libby Welch (BR) 141.
Ian Armitage: 19 (BR); 81 (TL), (BL), (R);
119 (TR); 120; 125 (BL).
T. C. Bird: 7 (T); 17; 20; 21; 23 (TR); 71;
114; 122; 138–139; 142; 143 (BL);
144; 156.
Jane Courtier: 107; 127.

GAP Photos: Friedrich Strauss 10–11,
12, 13, 83, 105; Gary Smith 14 (BL),
97–98; Victoria Firmston 15; Elke
Borkowski 16, 18 (TR), 106; Mark
Bolton 22; Graham Strong 23 (BL);
Lynn Keddie 27, 85; Lee Avison
112–113; Maxine Adcock 121 (BL),
148; Elke Borkowski 124; Graham
Strong 140 (BL); Michael Howes 141
(BL); Claire Davis 141 (BM).
GWI: L. Cole 133.
Getty Images: Heinrich van den Berg
101.
Harrod Horticultural: 19 (TL).
istockphoto: 135.

LDI: David Murray 75; Sharon Pearson
110; David Murray 111, 126,136, 137.
Photolibrary: Friedrich Strauss 5; David
Cavagnaro 14 (TR); Francesca Yorke
100; Friedrich Strauss 157.
Denis Ryan: 121 (TR).
Shutterstock: valda 102; Nic Neish
103, 119 (BL); macka 130 (BL); Anne
Kitzman 130 (BR); Norman Chan
131 (BL), (BM); Artography 131
(TR); Melinda Fawver 138; Yurok
139, 143 (TR); 145 (BL); marykai
145 (TR); Tatiana Markotra 146 (BL);
Shutterstock 147 (BL), (BM), 151;
Calek 155.

Mark Winwood: 2; 6; 7 (M), (B); 8–9;
24–25; 29; 31 (L), (TR), (BR); 33 (L),
(TR), (BR); 35; 37; 39 (L), (TR), (BR);
41; 43; 45 (L), (TR), (BR); 47; 48–49;
51 (L), (TR), (BR); 53 (L), (TR), (BR);
55; 57; 59; 61; 63; 65; 67; 69 (L), (TR),
(BR); 73 (L), (TR), (BR), 76–77; 79; 87
(RL), (BL), (R); 89; 91; 93; 95; (L), (TR),
(BR); 108; 109 (BL), (BM), (BR); 115;
116; 117; 118; 120; 125 (TR); 128
(BL); 129; 131 (BR); 132; 134; 146
(BM); 147 (BR); 149 (BL), (TR); 150;
152; 153; 154.
VegTrug.com: 18 (BL).

Acknowledgments

The author and Toucan Books would like to thank the following people and organizations for their assistance in the preparation of this book: Steve and Pam Barnett; Nick Hamilton and staff at Barnsdale Gardens; Burgon & Ball; Neil and Tracey Donnelly; Harrod Horticultural; Neil Miller at Hever Castle; Brian Knight at Knights Garden Centre, Nags Hall, Surrey; Tracy Collacott at Mr Fothergill's; Eduardo and Gary at StART SPACE, www.startspace.co.uk; Tom Sharples and Francijn Suermondt at Suttons Seeds; Colin Randel at Thompson & Morgan; Charles Tory; Patrick and Sue Tory; Jim Juby at Vegetalis; and Steve Mercer at *Which? Gardening*.

Hardiness across North America

Plants that survive freezing winters are called hardy, while those that succumb to cold weather are called tender. Plants are rated according to the coldest temperatures they can survive in, based on the climates across the continent, which have been divided into zones on a map.

The United States Department of Agriculture has compiled a hardiness zone map for both the United States and Canada, although Agriculture Canada has produced a slightly different version. These maps are divided into zones based on average minimum temperatures, with Zone 11 rated the warmest and Zone 1 the coldest. Each zone can grow plants from lower numbered zones. For example, if you live in Zone 4, you can include plants from Zones 3, 2, and 1 in your garden. For an interactive U.S. hardiness zone map, go to **http://www.usna.usda.gov/Hardzone/ushzmap.html**. Canadian readers can download a map from Agriculture Canada's website at **http://sis.agr.gc.ca/cansis/nsdb/climate/hardiness/intro.html**.

In addition, the American Horticultural Society has created a heat zone map, divided into 12 zones, based on the average number of days over 86°F (30°C), which are known as heat days. Zone 12 has the most heat days with an average of 210 heat days a year, while Zone 1 has no days above 86°F (30°C). You can download a pdf of the map at **www.ahs.org/pdfs/05_heat_map.pdf**.

Summer heat and humidity, and lack of winter chilling in warmer climates, may limit the ability of some plants to thrive. Because of this, and the fact that within each zone there are microclimates that can be colder or warmer, we suggest that you use the zones as a guide, but feel free to experiment with plants rated marginally hardy in your area.